Great S
and Ca

C000148188

First published in Great Britain by
Brian M. Leahy, 2006.

Copyright © Vicarious Books LLP.
Reprinted 2007.
All rights reserved.

A CIP catalogue record for this book
is available from the British Library.

ISBN 0-9547715-2-4

The moral right of the author has
been asserted.

Vicarious Books LLP,
PO Box 72, Minehead, TA24 9AL
Tel: 0131 208 3333
www.vicariousbooks.co.uk

Cover main picture:
Nicholaston Farm Caravan and
Camping Site, Penmaen.

Back cover:

Bay View Farm, St Martins,
Looe, Cornwall

Sango Sands Caravan and
Camping Site, Durness,
Sutherland

Queensberry Bay Caravan Park,
Annan, Dumfries & Galloway

The Lizard Peninsula, Cornwall

Muasdale Holiday Park in Argyll.

Printed and bound in England by
J. H. Haynes & Co. Ltd, Sparkford

Contents

Brian M Leahy first published this excellent guide in 2006.
He had travelled twice round the UK visiting every campsite
that had the potential to be a great site with a good view
of the sea. This reprint has a few minor amendments but
otherwise remains true to the original. Vicarious Books LLP
were pleased to accept Brian's kind offer to take over this
guide in 2007 and look forward to republishing it year on
year. Whilst every effort is taken to ensure the accuracy of
the information given in this guide, no liability can be
accepted by the authors or publishers for any loss, damage
or injury caused by errors in, or omissions from, the
information given. We gratefully accept site reports for the
campsites in this guide as well as others you may wish to
nominate. Please use the form at the rear of the guide and
make copies as required.

Vicarious Books LLP

One Stop Motorhome and Caravan Bookshop

Go Motorhoming Europe

If you've ever said I have always wanted one of those or want to find out everything you need to know, then this book will answer all your questions even those you did not know you needed to know. 'the Bible' Motorhome monthly.

ACSI Camping Card

There are other low season discount schemes but none rival the quantity and freedom of this no commitment guide. Buy the book it's as simple as that and camp across Europe for a maximum of €14 a night. The card presses out of the cover.

Guida Camper

It's a little known fact that both motorhomes and caravans can use the mostly free overnight parking facilities throughout Italy. This is a guide to 1500 stopovers marked on a quality 1:300000 Italian road map.

Go Motorhoming Stopovers France

This long awaited English guide features over 1000 aires, 500 of which were inspected in 2007. Aires de services are motorhome only overnight stopovers across France. Mostly provided by the community, they are the essence of motorhoming.

France Passion

Like a glass of wine, then why not spend a night at the vineyard where you can see, smell and taste the process. Over 1000 farms to chose from where motorhomes of all sizes can stop the night for free. UK agent, see www.france-passion.co.uk

Campsite Guides Galore

We specialise in importing campsite guides from Europe, so no mater where your going we've got it covered. We also stock the superb Caravan Club Europe Guides, Alan Rogers and a range of other British Guides.

Stopover guides for all of Europe

We specialise in importing stopover guides from Europe, so no mater where your going we've got it covered. Reise Mobile Bord Atlas for Germany, Guida Camper for Italy, Go Motorhoming Stopovers France, and Camperstop Europe for a general guide across Europe.

0131 208 3333   www.vicarious-shop.co.uk

Camping and Caravan Sites
by County and Post Town

County:
Cleveland
Members only

Postal town:
Hartlepool

Address:
Crimdon House Farm,
Hart Station,
Hartlepool,
Cleveland, TS27 3AA

Telephone number:
01429 272526

Ordnance Survey grid reference:
NZ-093-483-365

Directions:
From the A19 take the A179 to Hartlepool. At the third roundabout take the A1086 North for Blackhall/Horden. The site is on the right immediately past the green bridge, turn down farm lane that is easy to miss.

Facilities:
Normal C.S. facilities and a flushing toilet up two steps. There is a pub one mile away and shops in 1.25 miles. Hartlepool marina three miles away has a slipway.

Description:
A three-quarter of an acre level site close to a farm. This is a classic Camping and Caravanning Club C.S. in a lovely mown field. It has gorgeous views across the sea and all at an extremely modest £4.00 a night. The sea is only a quarter of a mile away accessible down a national cycle way. The site is also at the starting of an 11 mile coastal footpath north to Seaham harbour. Open all year and takes RV's.

County:
Cornwall

Postal town:
Boscastle

Address:
Lower Pennycrocker Farm,
St. Juliot, Boscastle,
Cornwall, PL35 OBY

Telephone number:
01840 250257

**Ordnance Survey
grid reference:**
SX-190-125-927

Directions:
Nearly three miles North East and one mile South West of
Tresparrett Posts. On the B3262. Turn West after half a
mile.

Facilities:
The showers and toilets were revamped 2006, also having
washing up sinks electric hook-up. Shops, pubs and a
slipway are two miles away in Boscastle. Padstow harbour
caters for larger boats.

Description:
A four acre, 40 pitch level cliff top site on a working dairy
farm in an absolutely beautiful setting. Not only does it
have good sea views but wonderful views over 15 miles to
Padstow and beyond. Access to the sea is about a ten
minutes drive. Being situated on the coastal path,
provides excellent walking with Cornwall's highest cliffs
close by. The fishing lakes are stocked with carp and
tench. This Site takes RV's and is open from Easter -
beginning October and has been awarded one pennon
from the AA.

County:
Cornwall

Postal town:
Boscastle

Address:
Trebyla Farm,
Minster, Boscastle,
Cornwall,
PL35 OHL

Telephone number:
01840 250308

Ordnance Survey
grid reference:
SX-190-119-922

Directions:
Leave A39 road to the B3263 9½ miles South of Bude signposted Boscastle. After 3 miles Trebyla Farm is on the right in 100 yards.

Facilities:
Toilets, showers, washing up sinks and electric hook-up. Shops are in Boscastle, a one mile 20 minute walk, there are also three pubs and a slipway for small craft. Padstow harbour caters for all boats.

Description:
A two acre part level 30 pitch site with grand views. This is a very nice traditional livestock farm with superb views along the coast and good bird watching. Footpaths lead to the coastal path in half a mile and down the stunning Valency valley, the cause of the Boscastle floods. Follow the beautiful valley to St Juliot's church and on to Boscastle. Open all year, weather permitting, but is not suitable for RV's.

County:
Cornwall
Members only

Postal town:
Boscastle

Address:
Trewannion Farm,
Lesnewth, Boscastle,
Cornwall, PL35 0HP

Telephone number:
01840 261241

Ordnance Survey grid reference:
SX-190-137-904

Directions:
Turn right off the A39 Bude to Camelford road half a mile past the B3262 road at the junction signposted Lesnewth, St. Juliot Church. The site is on the right in one and a half miles.

Facilities:
Normal C.L. There is a Co-op at Camelford, a six mile, 10 minute drive and a pub is three miles, 5 minutes by car.

Description:
There is a panoramic view of the sea although it is three miles away. The site is on a working dairy farm, occupying one and a half acre gently sloping paddock. A wonderful classic C.L, that has invited campers for 30 years. This site is in the very best of the Cornish countryside that also looks down the Valency valley, the cause of the Boscastle floods. Walkers can follow the beautiful valley one a half miles to St Juliot's church and on to Boscastle, have lunch and make the return in five and a half hours. Winter visitors can park on a concrete area. This site does not take RV's.

County:
Cornwall
Non members welcome

Postal town:
Bude

Address:
Bude Camping and
Caravanning Club Site,
Gillards Moor,
St. Gennys, Bude,
Cornwall, EX23 0BG

Telephone number:
01840 230650

Website:
www.campingandcaravan
ningclub.co.uk

**Ordnance Survey
grid reference:**
SX-190-176-943

Directions:
From the North on A39 and the site is on the right in a
lay-by 9 miles from Bude.

Facilities:
Toilets, showers, laundry and a play area, washing-up
sinks, chemical disposal point, 16 amp electric hook-ups
and fully accessible toilet and shower. There is also a
very nice children's play area and a dog walk.

Description:
A Camping and Caravan Club Club site with a superb
view of the sea it is the perfect base to explore North
Cornwall's wild and rugged coastline. The problem with
perfection is that these sites are practically perfect.
Access to the sea is about a ten minute drive to
Crackington Haven.

County:
Cornwall

Postal town:
Bude

Address:
Penhalt Farm Holiday
Park, Widemouth Bay,
Poundstock,
Bude, Cornwall,
EX23 ODG.

Telephone number:
01288 361210

E-mail:
info@penhaltfarm.co.uk

Webite:
www.penhaltfarm.co.uk

**Ordnance Survey
grid reference:**
SS-190-194-003

Directions:
From Bude take the A39. In 4 miles take second road
signposted, Widemouth Bay onto Widemouth Hotel then
take the road sign posted Millook and site sign. The
entrance to the site is about 2/3 miles on your left.

Facilities:
Showers, toilets, and Disabled WC, washing up sinks,
laundry and hook-up. The play area and games room are
all features that make this a 3 star tourist board site.
There is an onsite shop and Bude is five miles, 10 minute
drive. Widemouth Manor pub is one mile.

Description:
A delightful working farm on a hill overlooking the sea.
The eight acre camping field is slightly sloping with
some level pitches but all 100 of them have views of the
sea. A most enjoyable site, good for a stopover or a long
idle rest. The site entrance is on the coastal path and it
is a 6 minute walk to the cliff edge and 30 minute walk
to a sandy beach. This site does not take RV's.

County:
Cornwall

Postal town:
Hayle

Address:
Beachside Holiday Park,
Hayle,
Cornwall, TR27 5AW

Telephone number:
01736 753080

Website:
www.beachside.co.uk

**Ordnance Survey
grid reference:**
SW-203-558-388

Directions:
Leave the A30 into the Hayle exit at the large roundabout and take the Hayle road. Turn right by the putting green and follow the signpost to Phillack and Towans Beaches. Follow the brown tourist signs to site.

Facilities:
Free toilets and showers, dish washing. A Swimming pool. A family bar, a games room, launderette, adventure play ground and a shop.

Description:
A 20 acre gently sloping field built out of an amazing complex of sand dunes that any child would love to play within. It has some level pitches many with views of the sea and all with views over the countryside.

County:
Cornwall

Postal town:
Kennack Sands

Address:
Chy Carne Camping,
Kennack Sands,
Near Helston, Cornwall,
TR12 7LX

Telephone number:
01326 290200

E-mail:
enquiries@camping-cornwall.com

Webite: www.camping-cornwall.com

Ordnance Survey grid reference:
SW-204-725-164

Directions:
On the B3293 St. Keverne road. After passing Goonhilly Earth Station, take the first unclassified road on the right signposted Kennack Sands. Proceed for three miles to T-junction in Kugar. Turn left and Chy Carne is on the left.

Facilities:
The toilet and shower block were renovated in 2006, there are washing up sinks and a laundry. Electric hook up and a play area help make this an AA Three Pennant site. Kennack Sands Inn is two minutes walk, and there is a shop onsite and at Bruan Minor in one mile. Boats can be launched at Kennack sands, a one-minute drive.

Description:
This is a part level part gently sloping site one acre of which is set aside for tourers, in total 22 vans and 80 tents are accommodated. There are stupendous views across the sea and along the Cornish coast. Set in an area of outstanding natural beauty on the Lizard Peninsula, peace and tranquillity, what more could one wish for. This site takes RV's and is open Easter to end October.

County:
Cornwall

Postal town:
Land's End

Address:
Trevedra Farm, Sennen,
Penzance, Cornwall,
TR19 7BE

Telephone number:
01736 871818

E-mail:
trevedra@btconnect.com

Website: www.cornwall
farwest.co.uk/trevedra.htm

**Ordnance Survey
grid reference:**
SW-203-369-274

Directions:
From Penzance turn right off the A30 two hundred yards past the B3306 junction and the site is in three quarters of a mile.

Facilities:
Toilets including disabled and shower, showers and two family washrooms, also has washing up sinks laundry. Hook-up 16amp. Wifi open access. Onsite shop and mobile snack bar in peak season. The Old Success pub at Sennen cove is two miles and there is also a slipway there.

Description:
A beautiful eight acre site based on a farm with open, dramatic views of the sea and cliffs. The sandy beaches of Sennen (designated dog free) and Gwenver are only a 10 minute walk away making this an ideal family holiday spot. Bathing off this coastline can be dangerous but all beaches have lifeguards. Open Easter or 1st April - 31st October and RV's are taken with prior warning.

Photo from Site Owner

Photo from Site Owner

County:
Cornwall

Postal town:
Looe

Address:
Bay View Farm,
St. Martins, Looe,
Cornwall, PL13 1NZ

Telephone number:
01503 265922 or
07967 267312
Fax: 01503 265922

E-mail: mike@looebay
caravans.co.uk

Website: www.looebay
caravans.co.uk

**Ordnance Survey
grid reference:**
SX-201-274-545

Directions:
Leave A38 at Trerulefoot 7 miles West of Plymouth, take A374 for 1 mile. Turn right onto the A387 towards Looe. At Widegates take the B3253 to Looe then turn left after 1 mile at No Mans Land. Follow signs to the monkey sanctuary. At the entrance to the monkey sanctuary bear right, site in half a mile.

Facilities:
Toilets, showers, washing up sinks, laundry and 16amp hook up. Shops and a pub are found at Seaton Beach in 1.5 miles. Looe has a slipway in 3 miles.

Description:
A very tidy, level site on a working farm with stupendous views of the sea with the wonderful sound of waves on the beach and rocks. Set on two acres with pitches for 15 caravans and 12 tents. A group of friendly Shire Horses add to the ambience and you are assured a friendly welcome from the site owners. This is one of Brian's top ten sites and greatly admired by other writers. The coastal path passes the entrance with Millendreath Beach just a 10-minute walk. Open all year and takes RV's.

County:
Cornwall

Postal town:
Marazion

Address:
Kenneggy Cove Holiday Park, Higher Kenneggy, Rosudgeon, Penzance, Cornwall, TR20 9AU

Telephone number:
01736 763453

E-mail: enquiries@ kenneggy cove.co.uk

Website: www.kenneggy cove.co.uk

Ordnance Survey grid reference:
SW-203-562-286

Directions:
Three miles East of Marazion and 7 miles West of Helston on the A394 and just East of Rosudgeon where you turn South after ½ mile to site.

Facilities:
Toilets, showers, washing up sinks, laundry and hook up. Shop onsite and home cooked takeaway, with two pubs within 15 minutes walk. Marazion is three miles away and has a slipway.

Description:
A beautifully laid out attractive four acre 50 pitch site with level lawns, palm trees, picnic tables and wonderful views to the sea. The owners take so much care to keep it pristine and have been awarded a four star rose award. A twelve minute countryside walk takes you to the South West Coast Path and the very secluded white sands of Kenneggy beach. Not suitable for RV's. Open: April – October.

Photograph from the site owner.

County:
Cornwall

Postal town:
Mullion

Address:
Teneriffe Farm,
Predannack, Mullion,
Helston, Cornwall,
TR12 7EZ

Telephone number:
01326 240293

E-mail:
teneriffefarm@aol.com

Website:
www.cornishspirit.co.uk/
accommodation/english/
teneriffe_farm.htm

**Ordnance Survey
grid reference:**
SW-203-672-166

Directions:
From the A3083 eight miles South of Helston. Take the B3296 through Mullion towards Mullion Cove, about a quarter of a mile. Turn left, signposted Predannack. Site is on the left in approximately 1 1/4 miles.

Facilities:
Toilets, showers, washing up sinks, laundry and hook up. Shops and two pubs are 1 1/2 miles at Mullion. There is a slipway in 1 1/2 miles at Mullion cove.

Description:
This is an extremely tidy and well kept three acre 24 pitch touring site next to a working farm. Most pitches have superb views of the sea, some have hard standing. An absolutely excellent site run by two very nice people who take great pride and offer you wonderful views at a very reasonably prices. Mullion Cove is within easy walking distance. Mullion village is the largest in Cornwall offering numerous shops and pubs. Polurian beach is a 1 1/2 mile walk, you can drive 5 minutes to Polduh and 10 minutes to Kynannace beaches. Open: 1st April 31st October. RV's not taken.

County:
Cornwall
Caravan Club Members
only

Postal town:
Newlyn

Address:
Kemyel Crease, Paul,
Penzance, Cornwall,
TR19 6NP

Telephone number:
01736 731589

E-mail: ho@fenton66.
freeserve.co.uk

**Ordnance Survey
grid reference:**
SW-203-458-247

Directions:
From Penzance to Newlyn at Newlyn Bridge continue
onto the B3315 signposted Porthcurno. In about 1 mile
after passing through the Village of Sheffield fork left
signposted Castallack. At right hand bend continue into
a "No through road" signed at end, bear left and the site
is in half a mile. Call at the farmhouse on your left.

Facilities:
Normal C.L. Shops are two miles at Newlyn, there is a
pub at Paul in 1.5 miles. Newlyn also has a slipway.

Description:
A level field with breath-taking views across open
countryside and Mounts Bay to the Lizard peninsula.
This is not a serviced camping site but a wonderful,
peaceful and tranquil place that used to be a farm. Now
the only diesel engines heard are those of passing
fishing boats. So free of light pollution even if you're not
a stargazer you will feel you're on the roof of the world.
Open 1st June 30th September and takes RV's.

County:
Cornwall
Non members welcome

Postal town:
Newquay

Address:
Tregurrian Camping and
Caravanning Club Site,
Tregurrian,
Near Newquay,
Cornwall,
TR8 4AE

Telephone number:
01637 860448

**Ordnance Survey
grid reference:**
SW-200-847-654

Directions:
From the A3059 to Newquay. One and a half miles after
passing a service station turn right to Newquay Airport.
Continue to a junction where you turn left to Tregurrian
and follow the signs to Watergate Bay.

Facilities:
Toilets, showers, laundry and a play area, washing-up
sinks, chemical disposal point and a 16 amp electric
hook-ups and fully accessible toilet and shower.

Description:
A spacious field bordered with hedges with space for
ninety pitches, a number of which have hard-standings.
There are distant views of the sea from some pitches and
the site has been awarded four stars from the British
Tourist Board and three pennons from the A.A. A nice site
with good views and up to the normal high standards of
the Camping and Caravanning Club. The site is just three
quarters of a mile away from Watergate Bay, a glorious
sandy beach which is a haven for water sport lovers and
there are pretty coastal walks from the site to the beach.

County:
Cornwall

Postal town:
Padstow

Address:
Mother Ivey's Bay
Caravan Park,
Trevose Head, Padstow,
Cornwall, PL28 8SL

Telephone number:
01841 520990

E-mail: info@Mother
IveysBay.com

Website: www.mother
iveysbay.com

Ordnance Survey
grid reference:
SW-200-865-755

Directions:
From Wadebridge take the A389 North to Padstow, then the B.3276 to Newquay. Follow signpost to Mother Ivey's Bay.

Facilities:
Toilets, showers, hairdriers, dishwashing, launderette, shop, adventure play ground and a large play area. There are four payphones. The site has its own private sandy beach. No club but there is an off licence on site.

Description:
A twenty three acre site on Trevose Head mainly set to statics of which eleven acres are set to tourers providing one hundred pitches. The site is immaculately laid out with palm trees, fuchsias and flower borders. Many of the touring pitches have views of the sea. There are even some specially laid out super pitches. This a superb site and worth checking out its Web Page. Access to the sea could not be simpler as the site has its own private sandy beach.

County:
Cornwall

Postal town:
Portscatho

Address:
Trewince Farm,
Portscatho, Truro,
Cornwall, TR2 5ET

Telephone number:
01872 580430

E-mail:
info@trewincefarm.co.uk

Ordnance Survey grid reference:
SW-204-863-339

Directions:
From St. Austell take A390 towards Truro. Bear left on the B3287 to Tregony. From Tregony follow the signs to St. Mawes for seven miles to Trewithian and then turn left at the sign for Gerrans, Portscatho, Trewince Manor. Stay on this road, following signs for St. Anthony to Trewince Farm half a mile beyond Gerrans village.

Facilities:
Hook-ups, free shower and toilet block. Washing up sinks and coin operated laundry equipment. A restaurant, bar and swimming pool at the nearby Trewince Manor. Shops in a nearby village.

Description:
This five acre site adjacent to a working farm is in the middle of a make over but the touring site will stay on the higher part of it with good views across the countryside to the sea. On a slope but there are many level pitches. Towan Beach is within walking distance whilst Porthcurnick, Porthbeor, Pendower and Carne are but a short distance.

County:
Cornwall
Non members welcome

Postal town:
Sennen Cove

Address:
Higher Tregiffian Farm,
Sennen Cove Camping
and Caravanning Club
Club Site, St. Buryan,
Penzance, Cornwall,
TR19 6JB

Telephone number:
01736 871588

**Ordnance Survey
grid reference:**
SW-203-378-276

Directions:
Follow the A30 towards Lands End. Turn right onto the A3306 St. Just/Pendeen Road and the site is fifty yards on the left.

Facilities:
Has comprehensive ablutions including disabled. Hook up. Adventure play, and a large play area. Onsite shop with off-licence and more shops 2.5 miles away at St Merryn. Harlyn Bay Inn is one mile away. A slipway can be used at Padstow, four miles away.

Description:
The 23 acre park is set in an area of outstanding natural beauty on Trevose Head, adjoining its own private sandy beach. There are many static caravans for hire and these are set closest to the beach. The site is immaculately laid out with palm trees, fuchsias and flower borders. Many of the 100 touring pitches have views of the sea. This is a superb site having gained a British Tourist Board Rose award and BH & HPA David Belamy Gold. Open1st April – October 28th and takes RV's subject to pitch availability.

County:
Cornwall

Postal town:
St. Agnes

Address:
Beacon Cottage Farm
Touring Park,
Beacon Drive, St. Agnes,
Cornwall, TR5 0NU

Telephone number:
01872 552347

E-mail: beaconcottage
farm@lineone.net.

Website: www.beacon
cottagefarmholidays.co.uk

**Ordnance Survey
grid reference:**
SW-203-703-501

Directions:
From the A30 at Chiverton roundabout take the B3277 to St. Agnes. In 3 miles past Presingall Barns turn left at the mini roundabout signposted Chapel Porth. Follow brown tourism signs for one and a half miles.

Facilities:
Toilets, showers, 10amp hook up, washing up sinks and laundry. There is a small play area and onsite shop. Driftwood Spars pub is 1.5 miles and there is a slipway 1.5 miles away at Trevaunance cove.

Description:
A very spectacular view of the coast stretching across the bay to St.Ives. A beautifully maintained, immaculate site. The 70, individually numbered, pitches are set out in six small landscaped paddocks over four acres. Two of the paddocks enjoy beautiful sea and coastal views while the others are surrounded by trees, offering shelter for those who prefer it. Open 31st March – October 1st. This site does not take RV's.

County:
Cornwall
Members only

Postal town:
St. Agnes

Address:
St. Agnes Beacon
Caravan Club Club Site,
St. Agnes, Cornwall,
TR5 0NU

Telephone number:
01872 552543

**Ordnance Survey
grid reference:**
SW-203-705-502

Directions:
From the A30 turn right at Chiverton roundabout onto the B3277 signposted St. Agnes. In 3 miles you pass Presingall Barns on your right where you turn left at the mini roundabout signposted Chapel Porth. In 1¼ miles past the cross roads fork right into Beacon Drive. Do not turn into the road signposted to Chapel Porth. The site is the second on the right and the entrance is then in about ½ a mile.

Facilities:
C.L. facilities plus a laundry room but note:- **THERE IS NO TOILET AND SHOWER BLOCK**.

Description:
A six acre site arranged on several levels with views across the countryside and to the sea. Yet another wonderful little site up to the normal high standards of the Caravan Club situated at the foot of the Beacon with panoramic views of the Cornish coastline. Gently sloping and arranged on several levels, partly sheltered by gorse-topped banking, St Agnes is within walking distance for shopping and eating. Local beaches are excellent. Dogs are banned from Chapel Forth beach between Easter and October and bathing off this coastline can be dangerous.

County:
Cornwall

Postal town:
St. Agnes

Address:
Trevellas Manor Farm,
St. Agnes, Cornwall,
TR5 0XP

Telephone number:
01872 552238

**Ordnance Survey
grid reference:**
SW-203-731-517

Directions:
From Perranporth to St. Agnes on the B3285. Pass Trevellas airfield on the right, at Trevellas turn right for Blue Hill and Crosscombe. At the Crosscombe junction carry straight on. Trevellas Manor Farm is 100 yards in front of you.

Facilities:
Toilets and showers, hook-ups plus normal touring site facilities.

Description:
A spacious field of about six acres with panoramic views across countryside and the sea. A very peaceful and pleasant old fashioned site with glorious views and access to the sea is about a ten minute walk.

County:
Cornwall

Postal town:
St. Austell

Address:
Seaview International
Holiday Park, Boswinger,
Gorran, St. Austell,
Cornwall, PL26 6LL

Telephone number:
01726 843425

E-mail: holidays@
seaviewinternational.com

Website: www.Seaview
International.com

**Ordnance Survey
grid reference:**
SW-204-990-411

Directions:
If you're travelling from East of Exeter - Take the A30 Trunk road into Cornwall, passing Okehampton, Launceston and Bodmin. Turn left onto the A391 to St. Austell. Turn right onto the A390 and then take the B3273 - signposted Mevagissey. Drive past Pentewan and up the hill. At the very top, turn right at the crossroads, following the brown tourism signs and avoiding Mevagissey's narrow streets. Continue along this road for ten minutes.

Facilities:
The toilet and shower blocks are immaculate and even a large bathroom is provided plus another fully accessible one. There is also a laundry, baby changing facilities, a games room, tennis courts, a superb large well equipped play area in separate field away from any site traffic and a dog walk. All pitches have hook-ups. There is a barbecue area with take-away close to the swimming pool.

Description:
A beautifully laid out immaculately and well maintained commercial site with panoramic views to the sea. Suffice to say this is among my best ten sites in Britain and well worth a visit and the sea is only a gentle stroll away.

County:
Cornwall

Postal town:
St. Austell

Address:
Treveague Farm
Campsite, Gorran,
St Austell, Cornwall,
PL26 6NY

Telephone number:
01726-842295

E-mail: treveague.farm
@virgin.net

**Ordnance Survey
grid reference:**
SX-204-004-413

Directions:
From St. Austell take the B3273 road towards
Mevagissey. Go past Pentewan and at the top of the hill
turn right signposted Gorran. Go past Heligan Gardens
towards Gorran Churchtown, past the public house and
post office and turn right signposted Penare. After five
hundred yards turn left at the cross roads. The site is
half a mile straight ahead.

Facilities:
Toilet block.

Description:
A four acre partly level site on a working farm on the
brow of a hill with panoramic views across the sea and
rolling countryside. It is bordered by National Trust land,
and is part of "Cornwall Heritage". A very tidy and well
maintained site with flowers and bushes all over the
place with absolutely breathtaking views across the
rolling countryside and to the sea.

County:
Cornwall

Postal town:
St. Buryan

Address:
Treverven Touring
Caravan, Camping Site,
St. Buryan, Penzance,
Cornwall, TR19 6DL

Telephone number:
01736 810200

Website: www.chycor.co.
uk/camping/treverven/

**Ordnance Survey
grid reference:**
SW-203-410-238

Directions:
From Penzance take A30 to Catchall, then follow the
signpost to St. Buryan, straight through the village. Pick
up the B3315 road and look for the site sign. The site is
two and a half miles South of St. Buryan.

Facilities:
Toilets, showers, hook-ups, a mother and baby room plus
fully accessible toilets and showers. An on site mobile
shop/catering van calls in peak season.

Description:
A six acre level field with views to the sea adjacent to a
working farm. It is a large, immaculate site with very nice
views across open countryside and to the sea. The sort
of place which breeds people like the owner who lent us
the use of a toaster and kettle when we discovered that
our camping kit did not have such necessities.

County:
Cornwall

Postal town:
St. Ives

Address:
Trevalgan Family Camping Park, St. Ives, Cornwall, TR26 3BJ

Telephone number:
01736 796433

Ordnance Survey grid reference:
SW-203-490-401

Directions:
Approx one and a half miles from the centre of St. Ives on the B3306 coast road to Lands' End. Turn right at the signpost towards the second farm.

Facilities:
A large very nice play area, showers and toilets. An off licence and a take-away.

Description:
A small commercial five acre site with one hundred and twenty pitches in a spacious field with nice little touches such as picnic tables. It is beautifully kept and nicely laid out in individual pitches separated in many cases by small bushes and has wonderful views across the sea. The problem with this part of the world is that it is so beautiful that after writing about one site one does not want to just repeat the superfluities one had just used when writing about another site. Suffice to say this is a luxuriously appointed site, well set out and well maintained with very nice views of the sea. For the walker there are loads of what I think are referred to as "way marked walks" and the sea is just a short walk to the cliff top and coast path.

County:
Cornwall

Postal town:
St. Merryn

Address:
Higher Harlyn Park,
St. Merryn, Padstow,
Cornwall, PL28 8SG

Telephone number:
01841 520022

E-mail:
pbharlyn@aol.com

**Ordnance Survey
grid reference:**
SW-200-877-744

Directions:
From Padstow take the B3276 road South West. At the first cross roads South of St. Merryn turn right signposted Harlyn Bay. The site is one third of a mile on the left.

Facilities:
Toilets and showers, launderette. A shop in high season. Three bars and a restaurant, a heated swimming pool and children's play area.

Description:
A 30 acre site mainly set to tourers with 625 pitches most of which are level and some of which have sea views. A large "informal" site with some pitches having grand views of the sea which is within easy walking distance, about ten minutes.

County:
Cornwall

Postal town:
St. Merryn

Address:
Trethias Farm, Caravan
Park, Treyarnon Bay,
St. Merryn, Padstow,
Cornwall, PL28 8PL

Telephone number:
01841 520323

**Ordnance Survey
grid reference:**
SW-200-856-733

Directions:
Four miles West Southwest of Padstow on the B3276
road eleven mile from Newquay.

Facilities:
Farm shop, toilets, showers with a laundry room, hook-
ups. Bookings will only be accepted from people who are
prepared to recycle refuse at the site recycling point.

Description:
A very spacious level park with superb views across the
sea and along the Cornish coastline. The owner has
taken great care not to cram caravans in which means
that they all have good views and most of them have
views of the sea. To make sure that the park maintains
its peaceful atmosphere access is restricted to couples
and family groups. You will find that it is no accident
that this park has a David Bellamy conservation award
and a three star grading from the English Tourist Board.
The sea is a hop, skip and a jump to the coastal path, or
about one hundred metres with a maximum walk of four
hundred metres to Treyaron Bay.

County:
Cornwall
Non members welcome

Postal town:
Tintagel

Address:
Trewethett Farm Caravan
Club Club Site, Trethevy,
Tintagel, Cornwall,
PL34 0BQ

Telephone number:
01840 770222

**Ordnance Survey
grid reference:**
SX-200-074-897

Directions:
From the North East turn off onto the A30 via slip road onto the A395 signposted North Cornwall, Wadebridge, Camelford. In eleven miles at the T-junction turn right onto the A39 signposted Bude. In one mile turn left just before the transmitter. In 2½ miles at the T-junction turn right onto the B3266 signposted Boscastle. In about 2½ miles at the junction on the bend turn left onto the B3263. Site entrance is on right in about 2 miles.

Facilities:
Toilet/shower block, dish washing facilities and a laundry room.

Description:
A fifteen acre site on a cliff top overlooking Bossiney Cove maintained like a manicured bowling green developed in terraces so all of the pitches are level and most of them have superb and breathtaking views of the coast and the sea, Bossiney Cove a safe sandy beach. The coastal path is right next to the site leading to spectacular cliff top walks. Footpaths to Tintagel and Boscastle.

County:
Cumbria

Postal town:
Beckermet

Address:
Tarnside Caravan Park,
Tarnside, Braystones,
Beckermet, Cumbria,
CA21 2YL

Telephone number:
01946 841308

**Ordnance Survey
grid reference:**
NY-089-066-007

Directions:
Two miles South of Egremont on the A595. Turn at the sign for Braystones B5345 and follow Caravan Park signs.

Facilities:
Toilets, showers, excellent club house and comfortable lounge with a large screen T.V. The site has a train station on it which is on the main railway line from Carlisle to Barrow-in-Furness. The Gallery Restaurant has a good reputation for food cooked from local farms and does a traditional Sunday lunch.

Description:
A tidy well mown site with work going on all over the place to make it look attractive with tubs of flowers and daffodils. There are sea views, mountains in the far distance and that attractive tourist attraction. This is very attractive site on the fringes of the Lake District where there are views of the Irish Sea and South West Scotland and the most glorious sunsets imaginable. There must have been a remarkable amount of work carried out on this site to reach such very high standards and access to the sea is adjacent to the site, less than a two minute walk

County:
Cumbria
A Caravan Club C. L.
Members only

Postal town:
Grange-over-Sands

Address:
Middle Fell Gate Farm,
Lingwood Park,
Cartmel Road,
Grange-over-Sands,
Cumbria, LA11 7QA

Telephone number:
01539 532271

**Ordnance Survey
grid reference:**
SD-097-395-773

Directions:
Turn right off the B5277 Grange-Over-Sands-Greenodd at staggered crossroads on the outskirts of Grange-Over-Sands signposted Cartmel (Low Fell Gate Camping, Grange Fell Golf Club); in 700 yards. Call at the farmhouse on the left in 500 yards past a licensed site because you need an entry code to get into the site. The Middle Fell Gate Farm C. L. is on the right into a wood after a further 200 yards.

Facilities:
A tap.

Description:
There is a good road up to the touring area where there are hardstandings and superb sea views. The site is hidden away from the road, surrounded by trees and hedges and only about a fifteen minutes walk to the sea.

County:
Cumbria
Non members welcome

Postal town:
Ravenglass

Address:
Ravenglass Camping and
Caravanning Club Site,
Cumbria, CA18 1SR

Telephone number:
01229 717250

**Ordnance Survey
grid reference:**
SD-096-086-965

Directions:
From the A595 turn West for Ravenglass. The site is on the left before you enter the village next to the 30mph sign.

Facilities:
Toilets, showers, hairdrier, laundry room and a small shop, electric hook-ups, family shower room and fully accessible toilets and showers.

Description:
This is a five acre wooded site with level hard standings dotted among the trees and is very attractive to the eye. There is a peaceful feel about the site, even the rabbits just walk past you and do not run away. You can just see the sea from a few selected pitches. A particularly attractive site now run as a Camping and Caravanning Club Club site who have made a considerable investment in it.

The site is approximately three minutes walk to the village with its shop and pubs. The park is an ideal base to explore the hidden secrets of Eskdale, Wasdale, and Ennerdale. The Western lakes are a walkers' paradise with river and estuary walks to Scafell Pike, England's highest mountain and access to the sea is a five minute level walk.

County:
Devon

Postal town:
Berrynarbor

Address:
Napps Touring Holiday Park, Old Coast Road, Berrynarbor, North Devon, EX34 9SW

Telephone number:
01271 882557

Website:
www.napps.co.uk

Ordnance Survey grid reference:
SS-180-559-479

Directions: Two miles South West of Combe Martin three miles East of Ilfracombe on the A399. The site owner advises that you avoid Barnstaple as it is often congested and that you avoid the A39 coastal route from Minehead and Porlock as the road is narrow and extremely steep in parts.

Facilities: Electric hook-ups. A brilliant toilet and shower block with free showers, hairdriers and hand driers. Laundrette, shop and off licence. Heated swimming pool, tennis courts, children's paddling pool. Adventure playground, five-a-side football pitch, safe bathing at the nearby beach, bar and games room, café and take-away. Entertainment in high season.

Description: A wonderful, well cared for touring park right on the edge of Exmoor National Park where every pitch has a view of the sea. This is one of my ten best parks in Britain. When I spoke to the owner and said that I thought that this was one of the best views I had seen in Britain he replied, "Best views in Britain? This is the best view in Britain" and on reflection he was not very far out. The site is well maintained and very pretty. When I visited the site recently the toilet and shower block had just been refurbished and they were superb.

County:
Devon
Non members welcome

Postal town:
Brixham

Address:
Hillhead Caravan Club
Club Site, Holiday Park,
Hillhead, Brixham,
Devon, TQ5 0HH

Telephone number:
01803 853204

**Ordnance Survey
grid reference:**
SX-202-904-534

Directions:
On the A380 and 3 miles South of Newton Abbot turn right onto the ring road which is also the A380 signposted Brixham. In 7 miles at the traffic lights turn right onto the A3022 signposted Kingswear and Dartmouth. In two miles at the mini roundabout turn right and immediately fork left onto the B3205 signposted Kingswear and Dartmouth via Lower Ferry. The site entrance is on the left within a quarter of a mile.

Facilities:
Normal top rate facilities including a launderette, an outdoor swimming pool, skateboard ramp, shop, restaurant etc. etc.

Description:
This site offers some of the finest and certainly the most extensive list of facilities of the Club network and is set in twenty acres of Devon countryside with some pitches having views of the sea. Nearby Kingsbridge is an interesting old town well known for its excellent food, attractive buildings and an olde-worlde charm. Those who wish to swim should remember that bathing off the Cornish and Devon Coasts can be dangerous and particular note, must be taken of any local notices. It is two and a half a miles to the beach.

County:
Devon

Postal town:
Budleigh Salterton

Address:
Ladram Bay Caravan
Site, Otterton, Budleigh
Salterton, Devon,
EX9 7BX

Telephone number:
01395 568398

**Ordnance Survey
grid reference:**
SY-192 096-851

Directions:
Two miles North of Budleigh Salterton on the B3178
where you turn East after two miles to Ladram Bay.

Facilities:
A safe private beach with a slipway, shops, amusement
complex, launderette and indoor heated swimming pool
which is supervised at all times. A safe play area, crazy
golf, a children's club, a pub and family entertainment
during the high season.

Description:
This is a fairly large commercial site mainly set to statics
but with a couple of hundred caravan pitches and
pitches for tents. Some of the touring pitches are in level
fields but for a superb view others are on terraces carved
out of the hillside and children will love it. I thought that
the views from the upper terraces were lovely.

County:
Devon

Postal town:
Combe Martin

Address:
Sandaway Beach
Holiday Park, Combe
Martin Bay, Berrynarbor,
Ilfracombe, Devon,
EX34 9ST

Telephone number:
01271 866766 or
01271 883155

Website: www.johnfowler
holidays.com

**Ordnance Survey
grid reference:**
SS-180-571-471

Directions:
On the A399 a quarter of a mile North West of Combe Martin.

Facilities:
A toilet and shower block. Heated swimming pool. Private beach, restaurant, bar and night club with nightly entertainment. Amusement arcade. A children's club. Payphones.

Description:
This a commercial site where the tourers have no view of the sea. However, there are two tent camping fields with absolutely wonderful views over it. It may be possible to tow a touring caravan or drive a motor caravan into the camping field but it is practically impossible to get them out and it is just not economically viable to make it fit for tourers, more is the pity.

County:
Devon

Postal town:
Ilfracombe

Address:
Sunnymead Farm,
Mullacott, Ilfracombe,
Devon, EX34 8NZ

Telephone number:
01271 879845

E-mail: relax@mullacott
farm.co.uk

Website:
www.mullacottfarm.co.uk

**Ordnance Survey
grid reference:**
SS-180-499-442

Directions:
Take the A361 Barnstaple to Ilfracombe road and at Mullacott Cross take the B3343 road to Woolacombe. The site is approximately one mile on the right just past veterinary hospital.

Facilities:
A chemical disposal point, a family shower room, ladies and gents toilets, dishwashing facilities, a children's play area and picnic tables.

Description:
A very nice level one acre field adjacent to the road with a field next to it with horses. A good traditional site for use as a stop over or a longer break in the middle of stunning country and with sea views. There are pubs, restaurants and shops quite close. A golf range, clay pigeon shooting and a national cycle track nearby.

Library Picture

38

County:
Devon
A Caravan Club C. L.
Members only

Postal town:
Kingsbridge

Address:
Mollies Field, East
Prawle, Kingsbridge,
Devon, TQ7 2DD.
Bookings to Mrs. M. J.
Tucker, Wincot, East
Prawle, Kingsbridge,
Devon, TQ7 2DF

Telephone number:
01548 511422

E-mail: marilynjtucker
@hotmail.com

**Ordnance Survey
grid reference:**
SX-202-780-362

Directions:
Turn right off the A379 Kingsbridge-Dartmouth crossroads
at Carehouse signposted Prawle, East Prawle. Follow
signpost E Prawle for about five miles. Keep on the main
road into the village past the pond on the right. Keep right
on entering the village and pass the green on the left. The
site is on the left in about one hundred yards. Do not turn
at Frogmore as the road to Prawle is steep and narrow.

Facilities:
Water points and electric hook-ups to each pitch.

Description:
A three quarter of an acre C.L. with panoramic views of the
sea in an interesting little village with a couple of pubs and a
café. A shop opens from Easter until the end of September.
The village is in an area of Outstanding Natural Beauty, a
Coastal Preservation Area on the South Devon Coast and in
a site of Special Scientific Interest. An absolute paradise for
bird watchers. The local beaches are sandy and safe for
swimming and there are rock pools. There are also 11 miles
of footpaths and bridleways within the parish to explore. It
is less than a mile to a sandy beach.

County:
Devon
Members only

Postal town:
Kingsbridge

Address:
Slapton Sands Camping
and Caravanning Club
Site, Middle Grounds,
Slapton, Kingsbridge,
Devon, TQ7 1QR

Telephone number:
01548 580538

**Ordnance Survey
grid reference:**
SX-202-825-450

Directions:
On the A379 from Kingsbridge. The site entrance is a
quarter of a mile from the A379 beyond the brow of the
hill approaching Slapton.

Facilities:
Toilets, showers, laundry, a parent and baby room, a play
area, washing-up sinks, chemical disposal point, dog walk, 16
amp electric hook-ups and fully accessible toilet and shower.

Description:
A gorgeous five and a half acre site overlooking Start
Bay in beautiful rolling Devon countryside. The site
meets the normal very high standards of the Camping
and Caravanning Club and has a four stars British Tourist
Board award, a three pennons award from the A.A. and a
five star Loo of the Year Award. Suffice to say this was as
good as any Camping and Caravanning Club Site that I
have seen.

County:
Devon
A Caravan Club C. L.
Members only

Postal town:
Lynton

Address:
Caffyns Farm, Lynton,
Devon, EX35 6JW

Telephone number:
01598 753524

**Ordnance Survey
grid reference:**
SS-180-691-481

Directions:
Turn right off the A36 Tiverton to Barnstaple road at the roundabout onto the A399 road signposted Combe Martin and Blackmoor Gate. In 11 ³/₄ miles at Blackmoor Gate turn right onto the A39 road signposted Lynton and Lynmouth. In 5 ¹/₂ miles at Caffyns cross roads turn left signposted Caffyns and in 50 yards keep left and after half a mile turn right into the farm road. The site entrance is on the left in 350 yards.

Facilities: Basic C.L.

Description:
A beautiful site in two fields of about two acres each and is a part of a working farm. An absolutely perfect C.L. in the best traditions with no frills but with superb views across open countryside and the sea to the Welsh coast. This is a real working farm with a real down to earth working farmer born and bred in Devon. It is in a lovely walking area with many beauty spots. Pony trekking is available half a mile away and it is one of my best ten sites in Britain and one of the few sites where I would be happy to stop for a few weeks. One can feel the peace and tranquillity. It is a trifle off the beaten track but it is really worth going to have a look at. Many of the visitors to this Caravan Club C.L. have been returning for over 20 years.

County:
Devon

Postal town:
Paignton

Address:
Beverley Park Caravan &
Camping Site,
Goodrington Road,
Paignton, Devon, TQ4 7JE

Telephone number:
01803 843887

**Ordnance Survey
grid reference:**
SX-202-886-576

Directions:
South of Paignton 2 miles on A380 road into
Goodrington Rd.

Facilities:
Bars, restaurant, café, shops, sauna, indoor and outdoor
heated swimming pools, tennis courts, playground and
an indoor soft play area There are superb toilet blocks, a
launderette, electric hook-ups and fully accessible toilets
and showers. To add to this package there is all sorts of
entertainment laid on for adults and children.

Description:
A camping and caravan park with everything, very well
laid out, extremely tidy and with good views across Tor
Bay. The site is divided into a number of fields with
hedges and flower borders. Paignton is where one is
entering the golden beach land of Devon and many of
the touring pitches on this site give a good view of the
Bay. The sea is about a twenty minute walk.

County:
Devon

Postal town:
Sidmouth

Address:
Salcombe Regis,
Camping and
Caravanning Site,
Sidmouth, Devon,
EX10 0JH

Telephone number:
01395 514303

E-mail: contact@
salcombe-regis.co.uk

Website:
www.salcombe-regis.co.uk

**Ordnance Survey
grid reference:**
SY-192 149-892

Directions:
From the A3052 Exeter/Lyme Regis road, turn South
West at top of Trow Hill, one and a half miles South East
of Sidmouth and it is seven hundred yards to the site.
Do not take your caravan into Sidmouth itself.

Facilities:
Hook-ups, free hot water, showers and dishwashing
Launderette, ironing facilities and hairdriers. A fully
accessible family bathroom and a superb children's play
area. Plenty of picnic tables.

Description:
A remarkable site in open countryside with views to the
sea from the tented area and it is not surprising that it
has received so many awards. An absolute revelation in
caravan and camping site management with an extremely
helpful receptionist. The park is situated on the edge of
the picturesque village of Salcombe Regis less than a
mile from the sea, about a twenty five minute walk across
fields. All in all a most enjoyable place to stay and made
more enjoyable by very reasonable site fees.

County:
Devon

Postal town:
Teignmouth

Address:
Coast View Holiday
Park, Torquay Road,
Shaldon, Teignmouth,
Devon, TQ14 0BG

Telephone number:
01626 872392

**Ordnance Survey
grid reference:**
SX-202-935-717

Directions:
From the M5 to Exeter, follow signpost to Torbay, then
Teignmouth. Cross Shaldon Bridge over the River Teign.
The site is just above the hill, overlooking the coast.

Facilities:
Shower block, free, launderette, and shop. Separate
toddlers and adults indoor heated swimming pools.
Adventure play area, club house and bar. Very nice
restaurant serving the best apple pie I have ever eaten.

Description:
A very tidy twenty acre site most of which is set to
statics on level ground but there is also space for twenty
eight touring pitches and one hundred tents in well
defined pitches bounded by trees and bushes. The site
enjoys panoramic views across Tor Bay, Teignmouth,
Lyme Bay and Portland Bill. I have to say that I thought
this was a most enjoyable place to stay, peaceful,
wonderful views, congenial restaurant and lots of
interesting places to visit.

County:
Devon

Postal town:
Woolacombe

Address:
Damage Barton
Camping and
Caravanning Club Site /
Caravan Club Site,
Mortehoe, Woolacombe,
North Devon, EX34 7EJ

Telephone number:
01271 870502

E-mail: info@damage
barton.co.uk

Website: www.damage
barton.co.uk

**Ordnance Survey
grid reference:**
SS-180-471-451

Directions:
From the M5 leave at Junction 27 and follow signs for Barnstaple via the North Devon Link road and the A361. If you wish to avoid Barnstaple turn right off the A361 at Aller Cross roundabout onto the A399 signposted Combe Martin, Woolacombe and Lynton. In about fifteen miles turn left onto the A3123 to Mullacott Cross roundabout then as from Barnstaple above. Do not attempt to approach from the South on the B3231 as the route is quite unsuitable.

Facilities:
Hook-up, toilet and shower block and fully accessible toilet and shower. Baby and toddler washroom, washing up and laundry facilities, wet suite washroom. Bus Stop at site entrance with a service to Woolacombe, Ilfracombe and Barnstaple.

Description:
The site is part of a six hundred acre beef and sheep farm of which about ten acres have been set aside for one hundred and ten touring pitches and tents. Gently sloping but plenty of level spots and some hard standings. This is one of my best ten sites in Britain and a most beautiful site with wonderful views. One very good thing about this site is that they do not have those awful street lights all over the place on all night. Access to the sea is a thirty minute walk. It is well worth looking at the web page.

County:
Devon

Postal town:
Woolacombe

Address:
Easewell Farm Holiday Parc, Mortehoe, Woolacombe, Devon, EX34 7EH

Telephone number:
01271 870343

E-mail: goodtimes @woolacombe.com

Website:
www.woolacombe.com

Ordnance Survey grid reference:
SS-180-462-455

Directions:
From the junction of the A361 and B3343 at Mullacott Cross follow signpost for Woolacombe and Mortehoe. In half a mile turn Right at Turnpike Cross signposted Mortehoe. Site is on the right in one mile.

Facilities:
Hook-ups, toilet/shower blocks. Outdoor and indoor heated swimming pools. Fully affiliated golf club, old fashioned skittles and indoor bowling. Cross the road to Twitchen Parc, a sunshower solarium, night club, restaurant, bar/take-away, supermarket and nightly entertainment.

Description:
This must be the jewel in the crown of Woolacombe Bay Holiday Parcs because it is absolutely beautiful with grand views and space for 116 pitches with hardstandings. 113 grass pitches with electric hook-up and 106 grass pitches without an electric hook-up. It is immaculately kept with wonderful views to the sea. I thought that this was an absolutely beautiful site with superb views. Everything about it was superbly maintained and it was easy to see the effects of a new management team.

County:
Devon

Postal town:
Woolacombe

Address:
Europa Park, Beach
Road, Woolacombe,
Devon, EX34 7AN

Telephone number:
01271 871425

E-mail: holidays@
europapark.co.uk

Website:
www.europapark.co.uk

**Ordnance Survey
grid reference:**
SS-180-464-438

Directions:
On the B3343 road. The site is on the right hand side of
the main road by a garage approximately one mile from
Woolacombe.

Facilities:
An immaculate toilet and shower block. A club house on
site. An indoor heated swimming pool. Hard-standings,
electric hook-ups and a pet exercise area.

Description:
A wonderful little site of twelve acres beautifully laid out
in terraces so there are plenty of level touring pitches
with views over Barnstaple Bay and Lundy Island.
Obvious care had been given to the way it was laid out
and maintained. The sea is a ten minute walk down hill
so you have to climb back up again.

County:
Devon

Postal town:
Woolacombe

Address:
North Morte Farm
Caravan & Camping Park,
Mortehoe, Woolacombe,
North Devon, EX34 7EG

Telephone number:
01271 870381

E-mail: holidays@north
mortefarm.co.uk

Website: www.north
mortefarm.co.uk

**Ordnance Survey
grid reference:**
SS-180-461-457

Directions:
Four and a half miles South West of Ilfracombe. Turn
North West of the B3343 road at Turnpike Cross, it is 2
miles to the site which is 500 yards from the centre of
Mortehoe village. Do not attempt to approach from
Woolacombe if you are towing or are driving a large
motor caravan.

Facilities:
Great toilet/shower block, hairdriers. Laundry room,
tumble driers, ironing facilities. Site shop, off-licence,
Calor and Camping gas. Families and couples only. No
single sex groups of three or more and no large groups
in excess of six

Description:
A wonderfully well kept site of twenty five acres with
statics and twenty five touring caravan pitches and one
hundred and fifty tent spaces. This is the sort of site
where one could stay for a month and still find
something different to look at every day. It is absolutely
beautiful and well worth sending for a brochure.

Library Picture

48

County:
Dorset

Postal town:
Bridport

Address:
Golden Cap Caravan
Park, Seatown,
Chideock, Bridport,
Dorset, DT6 6JX

Telephone number:
01308 422139

E-mail:
holidays@wdlh.co.uk

Website:
www.wdlh.co.uk

**Ordnance Survey
grid reference:**
SY-193 423-920

Directions:
On the A35 through Chideock and turn South to
Seatown opposite the church. The site is approximately
one mile on the left.

Facilities:
A shop, showers, toilets, a laundry room, a play area,
hook-ups, tourist information and a fishing lake.

Description:
This is a twenty three acre park mainly set to statics but
with over a hundred touring pitches, most with very
good sea views and an additional camping area is
opened in the summer period. This is one of a number
of parks operated by West Dorset Leisure Holidays all to
a very high standard. The actual site and its facilities
were immaculate but the whole reason for my visit was
to see the sea and the views from the touring area were
wonderful. Access to the sea is a few minutes' walk.

County:
Dorset

Postal town:
Eype

Address:
Eype House Caravan
Park, Eype, Bridport,
Dorset, DT6 6AL

Telephone number:
01308 424903

E-mail: enquiries@
eypehouse.co.uk

Website:
www.eypehouse.co.uk

Ordnance Survey
grid reference:
SY-193 446-912

Directions:
The site is not licensed for touring caravans. One and
a quarter miles West of Bridport on the A35. Take the
turning South to Eype and drive through the village
towards the sea.

Facilities:
Toilets, hot and cold water, showers, hair driers,
launderette. No dogs in high season.

Description:
Four acres of sloping camping area but with absolutely
stupendously beautiful views. Includes some statics
available for hire. Space for twenty tents and a limited
number of smaller motor caravans. A quiet, un-crowded
site in an area of outstanding natural beauty with some
of the most awe inspiring views one would find in Britain.
It is just two hundred yards from the beach and has
extensive sea views and easy access to the unspoiled
beach. The village of Eype, unchanged by the years, has
a good "local".

County:
Dorset

Postal town:
Eype

Address:
Highland End Holiday
Park, Eype, Bridport,
Dorset, DT6 6AR

Telephone number:
01308 422139

E-mail-Address:
holidays@wdlh.co.uk

Website:
www.wdlh.co.uk

**Ordnance Survey
grid reference:**
SY-193-453-915

Directions:
1 1/4 miles West of Bridport. At the A35 turn South
towards Eype, take the third right then the entrance is
on your left.

Facilities:
Centrally heated toilet blocks, facilities for the disabled,
heated indoor swimming pool, solarium, gymnasium,
children's play area, tennis court, sauna/steam room,
restaurant, bar, hard-standings shop, tourist information
and pitch and Putt.

Description:
A 28 acre site largely set to statics but with 195 touring
and camping pitches, most with a view of the sea. There
are a large number of hard-standings. This is a real
quality site which others could do well to emulate
showing the high standard of management in the
pristine conditions of its facilities and grounds. The
views are absolutely stupendous and it is just five
hundred yards to a lovely unspoilt beach.

County:
Dorset
A Caravan Club C. L.
Members only

Postal town:
Kimmeridge.

Address:
Swalland Farm,
Wareham, Dorset,
BH20 5PD

Telephone number:
01929-480707

**Ordnance Survey
grid reference:**
SY-195-928-782

Directions:
Turn right off the A351 Wareham-Corfe Castle road opposite a cafe car park on the approach to Corfe Castle. In about a ¼ of a mile past a roundabout follow the sign-post to Kimmeridge. In about 3 miles, 1¼ miles past Church Knowle, turn left signposted Kimmeridge. Once in the village turn left into a private road to Smedmore House. In 1 mile bear right. Do not go to Smedmore House or Smedmore House Caravan Club club site on the right. Swalland farm C.L. is on the right in about half a mile.

Facilities:
Water and use of a toilet.

Description:
A sheltered field of about half an acre on a working farm, a trifle off the beaten track. This is an absolutely idyllic, classic C.L. where one can feel the silence. There are gorgeous views across the Isle of Portland made even more beautiful by a Western sunset.

County:
Dorset
Non members welcome

Postal town:
Wareham

Address:
Smedmore House
Caravan Site,
Kimmeridge, Wareham,
Dorset, BH20 5PB

Telephone number:
01929 480702

**Ordnance Survey
grid reference:**
SY-195-923-787

Directions: From the North on the A351. On approaching Corfe Castle, at the foot of Castle Hill turn right opposite the cafe and car park signposted Church Knowle and Kimmeridge. In 3¹/₄ miles, 1¹/₂ miles past Church Knowle turn left at the signpost, "Kimmeridge". In about 1 mile on the outskirts of Kimmeridge turn left, signposted, Smedmore House. In ¹/₂ a mile where Smedmore house is on the left turn right at the signpost to the site. Do not take any other turning after turning right at Kimmeridge as this takes you through a very narrow road and over a one in five hill.

Facilities:
Tap, disposal point and electric hook-up but **no toilet block.**

Description: A four acre Caravan Club Club site most of which is slightly sloping sheltered by trees on one side and hedges on the other surrounded by farmland within an area of Outstanding Natural Beauty that includes part of the World Heritage Coastline. Clavell Tower can be seen from one side of the site and the Purbeck Hills on the other. Kimmeridge Bay which is a part of the Smedmore Estate is famous for fossils, fascinating geological strata and rock pools. There is wind surfing and a slipway within close distance.

County:
Dorset

Postal town:
West Lulworth

Address:
Durdle Door Holiday Park, West Lulworth, Dorset, BH20 5PU

Telephone number:
01929 400352

Website: www.lulworth.com/holiday/holiday park.htm

Ordnance Survey grid reference:
SY-194-812-809

Directions:
Five miles West of Wareham at Wool on the A352 turn South on B3071 to West Lulworth. The site is one mile West of the village.

Facilities:
Good toilet and shower blocks, shop, bar and a take-away. There is also a very nice children's play area.

Description:
This is a large forty five acre commercial site impeccably maintained and with spaces for thirty five touring vans and tents. I've known this site for nearly fifty years since I first came here to the Royal Armoured Corps Gunnery Instructors' Training School. Durdle Door Holiday Park was then a slap happy but comfortable little site. Weld Enterprises Ltd. who own it must have spent a fortune in the last few years bringing the standards of the site up, and the views are stupendous. You can walk down the hill to the sea but you need to be reasonably fit to be able to walk back up it.

County:
Dorset

Postal town:
Weymouth

Address:
Pebble Bank Caravan
Park, 90 Camp Road,
Weymouth, Dorset,
DT4 9HF

Telephone number:
01305 774844

E-mail Address:
info@pebblebank.co.uk

**Ordnance Survey
grid reference:**
SY-194-657-776

Directions:
Turn Right off the A354 Weymouth-Portland road at the
mini roundabout onto the B3156 Wyke Road. In about 1
mile at a right hand bend just past church into Camp
Road, the site is on the left in 5 hundred yards.

Facilities:
Toilet and shower block, laundry facilities with a
washer/drier machine and an iron. Electric hook-ups. An
outdoor children's play area and a bar.

Description:
A large commercial site with one hundred holiday homes.
Three acres are set aside for touring caravans and motor
caravans and there is a one acre field set aside for tents.
A pleasant site very well set out and with wonderful
views across Lyme Bay, Portland and Chesil Beach.

County:
Dorset
A Caravan Club C. L.
Members only

Postal town:
Weymouth

Address:
Windridge, 481
Chickerell Road,
Weymouth, Dorset,
DT3 4DQ

Telephone number:
01305 779268

**Ordnance Survey
grid reference:**
SY-194 646 797

Directions:
On L of B3157 Weymouth-Abbotsbury road.

Facilities:
Normal for a C.L. but what a view. The site is on the bus route to Weymouth every 15 minutes and is also on the Jurassic coastal bus link every 30 minutes to Exeter and pool.

Description:
A long sloping field but with level pitches and hardstandings on the bottom part but when you get to the very top you have a panoramic view across Weymouth Bay, the town and surrounding countryside which is part of the Jurassic Coast World Heritage Status Coastline. The site is neatly mown and very tidy. It was a remarkable surprise to drive off the main road leading out of Weymouth and find such an unusual and attractive C. L. with such stupendous views perched right at the very top of a hill where one can park in near total peace and isolation. You do need a car to drive to the sea but it is only a three mile drive to a sandy beach in Weymouth.

County:
Essex

Postal town:
Mersea Island

Address:
Fen Farm Caravan &
Camping Site,
East Mersea, Colchester,
Essex, CO5 8UA

Telephone number:
01206 383275

**Ordnance Survey
grid reference:**
TM-168-058-144

Directions:
From Colchester take the B1052 road for seven miles
then East on an unclassified road for about three miles
taking a left fork as you come onto the island. Follow the
road to the Dog and Pheasant then take the first turning
right.

Facilities:
Good toilets and showers at no extra cost with special
toilet facilities for the disabled. There is also a baby-
changing unit and a nearby pub that serves food.

Description:
This was once a working farm and it now has two large
very nicely set out fields with panoramic views of the sea
devoted to well set out touring pitches of which there
are one hundred and twenty. A lot of time, money and
thought has been committed to developing this site with
loads of shrubs, bushes and trees planted. There are
many walks nearby and if you really feel fit you could
walk the sixteen miles round the island. Parts of the site
meet the beach.

County:
Gloucester
A Caravan Club C. L.
Members only

Postal town:
Aust

Address:
Cliff Farm, Aust, Bristol,
Gloucester, BS35 4BG

Telephone number:
01454 632400

**Ordnance Survey
grid reference:**
ST-172-565-891

Directions:
Leave the M48 at Junction one onto the A403
Avonmouth road and in one hundred yards turn right
across the dual carriageway. In about one hundred and
fifty yards past a C. L. on the left turn right over a cattle
grid into the drive. The site entrance to Cliff Farm is at
the end.

Facilities:
Normal for a C. L. but with basic toilet and showers and
electric hook-ups.

Description:
What a fascinating little place to find. A wonderful little
C.L. of about one acre on a working farm with views over
the Bristol Channel at what used to be a ferry. A
traditional C. L. on a working farm yet with views over
the estuary leading to Bristol and with views of the two
bridges to Wales which are great at night when one can
observe the lights of all the vehicles going to and from
Wales. Although not specifically a site with a view of the
sea, it is close enough, being an estuary.

County:
Hampshire
A Caravan Club C. L.
Members only

Postal town:
Southampton

Address:
Stonehill Farm,
Calshot Road, Fawley,
Southampton,
Hampshire,
SO45 1DW

Telephone number:
02380 891442

Ordnance Survey grid reference:
SU-96 464-028

Directions:
Leave M27 at Junction 2 onto the A326 signposted Fawley. In about 11 miles at the end of the A326 turn left onto the B3053 road signposted Calshot Activity Centre. Within 1¾ miles, one hundred yards past the turn on left to Ashlett turn left into a track signposted Stonehill Farm.

Facilities:
Usual for C.L.

Description:
A homely site but with fascinatingly interesting views of Southampton Water and all the busy traffic that sails through it. Quiet and level with some small camping bays. I thought this was a lovely C.L. The fields surrounding it had horses and there was a glorious view of Southampton Water. A site that I like to return to and I have.

County:
Kent

Postal town:
Folkestone

Address:
Folkestone Camping and Caravanning Club Site, The Warren, Folkestone, Kent, CT19 6PT

Telephone number:
01303 255093

Website: www.camping andcaravanningclub.co.uk

Ordnance Survey grid reference:
TR-179-246-376

Directions: From the A2 or A20 join the A260 and follow the signs to the Country Park. At the roundabout follow Hill Road. At cross roads drive into Wear Bay Road signposted, "Martello Tower", site is the fifth on the left.

Facilities: Toilets, showers, laundry, fully accessible toilet and shower, family room, washing-up sinks, chemical disposal point, 16 amp electric hook-ups. A rather long and steep approach road so use your gear box.

Description: A superb site on four acres set into the side of a cliff with eighty level pitches very well distributed in small groups overlooking the sea. A perfect base if you are on your way to the Channel Tunnel. Four star British Tourist Board award, three A.A. pennons and a five star Loo of the year award. No caravans are permitted on this site due to planning restrictions. This is yet another idyllic Camping and Caravanning Club Club Site with absolutely glorious views across the sea as you would expect from a site perched on the edge of the cliff and it is only a short walk to the beach. This is a place I felt that I could really stay a few days longer so I did.

County:
Norfolk

Postal town:
East Runton

Address:
Woodhill Park, Cromer Road, East Runton, Norfolk, NR27 9PX

Telephone number:
01263 512242

E-mail: infon@woodhill-park.com

Website:
www. woodhill-park.com

Ordnance Survey grid reference:
TG-133-198-428

Directions:
Off the A148 one and a half miles South of Sheringham Norfolk.

Facilities:
What I would call, "Camping and Caravanning Club" standard toilets, showers, washing up facilities and a launderette, a nice children's play area and, if that is not enough, an indoor heated swimming pool.

Description:
Thirteen acres are set aside for tourers giving a total of 394 pitches and 100 extra large multi-serviced pitches in this very pleasantly set out, immaculately maintained caravan park. A very impressive site right up in the air overlooking the sea but close enough to walk into the nearby village and with that invaluable asset to any business, a very helpful reception. The sea is a ten minute walk.

County:
Norfolk
A Caravan Club C. L.

Postal town:
Holt

Address:
The Shieling, Holt Road,
Cley Next The Sea,
Holt, Norfolk,
NR25 7TX

Telephone number:
01263 740628

**Ordnance Survey
grid reference:**
TG-133-052-429

Directions:
Turn off the A148 into Holt. In 100 yards at signpost
Cley turn left. The site is on the left in about three miles
just after Cley Nurseries.

Facilities:
Normal C. L. facilities plus toilets and showers in 2006.

Description:
The site is a classic C.L. in a level field of about one acre
with panoramic views to the sea and across the Glaven
Valley. A really nice site run by a very nice couple. Clean
and tidy with the first view of the sea since Withensea
some two hundred miles or so up North as there is a
very long set of sea defences running along the East
Coast. Access to the sea is under two miles by foot but
it is the view of the sea that I was looking for.

County:
Norfolk

Postal town:
Mundesley

Address:
Sandy Gulls Caravan
Park Ltd., Cromer Road,
Mundesley, Norfolk,
NR11 8DF

Telephone number:
01263 720513

**Ordnance Survey
grid reference:**
TG-133-299-377

Directions:
The site is 6 ½ miles South East of Cromer, 2 miles
North West of Mundesley on the B1159 coast road and
is best approached from Cromer.

Facilities:
Showers/washing up facilities at no extra charge and
electric and TV hook-ups. **The site does not cater for
children and teenagers.**

Description:
This is a lovely looking sixteen acre clean site with fifty
nicely set out pitches all with sea views. The site owners
quite correctly say in their brochure, "A superb cliff top
location." Yet another helpful reception which is always a
good introduction. The sea is within easy walking
distance of the beach.

County:
Northumberland
Non members welcome

Postal town:
Berwick-Upon-Tweed

Address:
Seaview Caravan Club
Site, Billendean Road,
Spittal,
Berwick-Upon-Tweed,
Northumberland,
TD15 1QU

Telephone number:
01289 305198

**Ordnance Survey
grid reference:**
NU-075-003-517

Directions: From the South on the A1 at the roundabout on the outskirts of Berwick turn right onto the A1167 signposted Scremerston-Tweed Mouth-Spittal. In one and a quarter miles at a roundabout turn right into Billendean Terrace signposted Spittal. There is a sign on the right pointing you towards the site which is in half a mile past a railway bridge.

Facilities:
Toilets, showers, laundry facilities and nearby shops.

Description: A six acre terraced site, part of which is sloping with one hundred and ten pitches mostly with hard-standings and a view of Berwick Harbour and the sea. This the northernmost Caravan Club Club site in England and not only does it offer the spectacular scenery of Northumberland but it is close enough to Scotland to nip across the border and explore. The site overlooks the river estuary and the bay, has wonderful views of Holy Island yet is only a 20-minute walk into Berwick with its Elizabethan ramparts, shops and places of interest. There are miles of unspoilt and safe beaches, small castles, pele towers and romantic ruins within close distance. The site is close to a sandy beach.

County:
Northumberland

Postal town:
Chathill

Address:
Beadnell Bay Camping
and Caravanning Club
Site, Beadnell, Chathill,
Northumberland,
NE67 5BX

Telephone number:
01665 720586

Website:
www.campingand
caravanningclub.co.uk

**Ordnance Survey
grid reference:**
NU-075-231-297

Directions:
Leave the A1 and follow the B1430, signposted, Seahouses
at Beadnell ignoring the signs for Beadnell village. The site
is just after the left hand bend after the village.

Facilities: Toilets, showers, chemical disposal point, a
laundry, washing up facilities. Close to a take-away.

Description: Non Camping and Caravanning Club
members are welcome at this large level site just across
the road from a pounding sea. **Only motor caravans
and tents are allowed to use this site.** The site has a
two star award from the British Tourist Board and two
pennons from the A.A. It is a gem, across the road from
sand dunes and sea with superb views made more
important by the scarcity of sites with a sea view in the
area. There is no electric hook-up but surely you can
manage for a day or so without one.

County:
Somerset.
Non members welcome

Postal town:
Minehead
**NO CARAVANS AS
THE ROAD IS FAR TO
STEEP AND BENDY
FOR THEM**

Address:
Minehead Camping and
Caravanning Club Site,
Hill Road, North Hill,
Minehead, Somerset,
TA24 5LB

Telephone number:
01643 704138

**Ordnance Survey
grid reference:**
SS-181-958-471

Directions:
From the A39 to Minehead towards the town centre. Turn right at the T-junction onto the dual carriageway taking the first left into Blenheim Road and the next left into Marlet Road. Keep left at the church following a narrow road for one mile to the site which is on the right.

Facilities:
Toilet/shower block, chemical disposal point, washing-up facilities, laundry, 16 amp hook-ups.

Description:
A site of about 3½ acres set at the top of a hill with trees and bushes dotted about in quiet and peaceful countryside giving spectacular views and easy access to Exmoor National Park. There are great views of Minehead, the surrounding countryside and the Bristol Channel. The site is generally sloping with a limited number of hard-standings for motor caravans and it is a great site for tents. Extremely well maintained, very well managed and good value for money with a four star British Tourist Board award and a three pennons A.A. award.

County:
Somerset

Postal town:
Watchet

Address:
Helwell Bay Holidays,
Watchet, Somerset,
TA23 0UG

Telephone number:
01948 631781

E-mail: www.helwellbay
@yahoo.co.uk

Website:
www.helwellbay.co.uk

**Ordnance Survey
grid reference:**
ST-181-077-432

Directions:
From Watchet take the coastal road to Bridgwater and the site is well signposted on your left as you leave Watchet.

Facilities:
Electric hook-ups and showers.

Description:
Helwell Bay is a traditional, old fashioned site of about one acre mainly set to statics but with a dozen or so pitches for tourers facing the Bristol Channel and with the West Somerset Steam Railway running just the other side of the fence from where the caravans are sited. This is a lovely old style site close to the small town of Watchet but also right on the edge of the Bristol Channel with views along the Somerset coast line. It is only eight minutes walk to the harbour town of Watchet which now has a modern marina. This is a good centre for touring the Quantocks or the Somerset coast and Watchet is an interesting old fashioned little place well worth spending time in. Only a couple of minutes to get down onto the beach.

County:
Somerset

Postal town:
Watchet

Address:
Warren Farm, Watchet,
Somerset, TA23 OJP

Telephone number:
01984 631220

**Ordnance Survey
grid reference:**
ST -181-084-432

Directions:
One and a half miles West of Watchet on the B3191.

Facilities:
A toilet and shower block.

Description:
This is an old established touring caravan and camping site on a two hundred and seventy five acre working farm with one hundred pitches, many of which are level and adjacent to a beach. A very nice, no frills, traditional camping and caravan site with grand views, peaceful and quiet and run by an on site owner who is a part of the land. Access to the sea is about a ten minute walk.

County:
Somerset
A Caravan Club C. L.
Members only

Postal town:
Williton

Address:
Staple Farm, West
Quantoxhead, Taunton.
Somerset, TA4 4EA

Telephone number:
01984 632495

**Ordnance Survey
grid reference:**
ST-181-109-415

Directions:
Turn left off the A39 Bridgwater to Minehead road at
West Quantoxhead immediately past the Windmill Inn.
Carry on up this road two hundred and fifty yards over
the cross roads. The farm is in fifty yards.

Facilities:
Normal C.L. facilities plus electric hook-ups.

Description:
The site is in a one acre field and is part of a working
farm with views over the Somerset countryside and the
Bristol Channel. I thought that this was a wonderful
traditional C.L. and I loved it. The site sits at the
Western end of the Quantock hills and is ideal for
walkers. Historic Dunster is seven miles away, the steam
train that runs between Bishops Lydeard and Minehead
can be joined at either Watchet or Blue Anchor Bay both
of which are only a short distance away and Exmoor is
on the doorstep. Access to the sea is couple of miles to
a shingle beach.

County:
Somerset

Postal town:
Weston-Super-Mare

Address:
Slimeridge Farm,
Touring, Park,
Links Road, Uphill,
Weston-Super-Mare,
Somerset, BS23 4XY

Telephone number:
01934 641641

**Ordnance Survey
grid reference:**
ST-182-312-587

Directions: Leave the M5 motorway at Junction 22 and drive North onto the A38 towards Bristol. Fork left onto the A370 road towards Weston-Super-Mare turning left at Weston Hospital, Grange Road. Continue and turn right at the roundabout. Take the first road left, Uphill Way, towards beach and follow the signs to the site which is adjacent to Weston-Super-Mare beach.

Facilities: Many of the pitches are booked for a whole season but there are eight grass pitches and ten pitches with hard-standings available. All have electric hook-ups and there is a superb, spacious toilet and shower block.

Description:
This a level site of about one acre and gives the impression of a Wild West corral where all the wagons gather in a circle only in this case the circle is composed of a rock wall which protects the park from the Bristol Channel when it gets rough. The park overlooks a golf course and the sandy beach which runs towards Weston-Super-Mare. This site has everything. It is next to a small village, it overlooks the Bristol Channel and yet it is close enough to walk into Weston-Super-Mare. The views are nice, the site and the facilities are clean and what more can one want. The sea is hop, skip and a jump onto the sandy beach.

County:
Suffolk

Postal town:
Corton

Address:
Azure Seas Caravan
Park, The Street,
Corton, Nr Lowestoft,
Suffolk, NR32 5HN

Telephone number:
01502 731403

E-mail:
infoazurseas@aol.co.uk

Ordnance Survey
grid reference:
TM-134-544-971

From the A12 two miles North of Lowestoft 7 miles
South of Yarmouth. Turn East at the end of a dual
carriageway along Corton Long Lane. The site is
opposite at the junction with "The Street", Corton next
to a pub called the Corton Hut.

Facilities:
Showers, toilets, electric hook-ups, a baby room and
washing and drying rooms.

Description:
This is a lovely unpretentious site where touring pitches
are set among the trees and if you like you can park up
directly overlooking the beach and I mean overlook the
beach. I really liked this site and the helpful warden. It
not only has breathtaking views but is next to a small
village for shops etc. Access to the sea is an easy walk or
if you like you could drop out of bed twenty feet or so
to the beach below.

County:
Suffolk
A Caravan Club C. L.
Members only

Postal town:
Kessingland

Address:
White House Beach
Caravan Club Club Site,
Kessingland, Lowestoft,
Suffolk, NR33 7RW

Telephone number:
01502 740278

**Ordnance Survey
grid reference:**
TM-156-534-857

Directions:
From the North follow the Kessingland by-pass to a roundabout at the end of the dual carriageway and turn left into Whites Lane, signposted Kessingland Industrial Estate, Wild Life Park. Continue into Church Road. In about one mile at the sea front, ignoring the "No Through Road" signs, turn right into Beach Road and the site is on the left.

Facilities:
Superb, as one would expect of the Caravan Club.

Description:
One part of this site is adjacent to a shingle beach and the other enclosed by willow and shrubs which means that there is a pitch to suit all tastes. In early summer the foreshore is a riot of colour with wild flowers, including the rare Yellow Poppy. Kessingland Wildlife Park is a short distance from the site. Lowestoft air show takes place each summer and Southwold is only a few miles away. For those who need to keep children amused Pleasure Wood Hills Theme Park is not far and one can take a day boat on The Broads and even go sea or river fishing. There is bird watching at Minismere and power boat racing on Dulton Broad. This site is without a doubt one of the nicest sites in the Caravan Club.

County:
Tyne & Wear

Postal town:
South Shields

Address:
Sandhaven Caravan Site, Bents Park Road, South Shields, NE34 7AB

Telephone number:
01914 566612 book at Tourist Information Centre.

E-mail: museum.tic@ s-tyneside-mbc.gov.uk

Website: www.visitsouth tyneside.co.uk

Ordnance Survey grid reference:
NZ-088-376-673

Directions: From the A19 or A19M follow the A194 towards South Shields then turn right onto the A3100. Continue straight along this road as far as you can go then turn left along the A183 Coats Road. Continue straight ahead at New Crown roundabout and the caravan park is approximately a quarter of a mile on the right hand side.

Facilities: Toilets, showers with hair driers. Electric hook-ups. Laundry facilities and a gas and gaz service.

Description: A beautifully maintained, high quality local authority site largely for statics but it does have fifty two touring pitches all approached from a tarmac perimeter road all with glorious views and close to the beach. It also has a sheltered area for tents. There are also three mobile homes available for hire. A beautifully laid out and well maintained site with the added advantage of a very happy and helpful site warden. It is not surprising that this site has a three star English Tourism Council award. The sea is a short walk across the road.

County:
Tyne & Wear.
A Caravan Club C. L.
Members only

Postal town:
Whitley Bay

Address:
Old Hartley Caravan
Club Site, Whitley Bay,
Tyne & Wear,
NE26 4R

Telephone number:
0191 2370256

**Ordnance Survey
grid reference:**
NZ-088-343-758

Directions:
Turn off the A19 about 2 miles North of the Tyne tunnel at junction with the A191 signposted Gosforth/ Whitley Bay follow tourist signs for St Mary's Island. At third roundabout turn left signposted Blyth. Pass Whitley Bay Holiday Park. In 2 miles at the Delaval Arms pub roundabout turn onto the cycle path and fork left in 50 yards to the site entrance. Watch carefully for the cycle path.

Description:
A superb Caravan Club Club Site with grand sea views. This most enjoyable Caravan Club site is, as usual, with superb facilities and a well cared for area. Access to the sea is within reasonable walking distance.

County:
Yorkshire

Postal town:
Driffield

Address:
Seaside Caravan Park,
Ulrome, Driffield, East
Yorkshire, YO25 8TT

Telephone number:
01262 468228

**Ordnance Survey
grid reference:**
TA-107-173-574

Directions:
On the A 165 Bridlington Hull road taking the B1242
road to Ulrome where you will see signs to the Seaside
Caravan Park.

Facilities:
Facilities for tourers such as a shower room and toilets
but with a supermarket and a launderette.

Description:
A comfortable homely site with good views of the sea. A
good, no-nonsense sort of site. Tidy, clean and with
good access to a soft sandy beach.

County:
Yorkshire

Postal town:
Filey

Address:
Filey Country Park,
North Cliff, Filey,
North Yorkshire,
YO14 9ET

Telephone number:
01723 513852

**Ordnance Survey
grid reference:**
TA-101-118-813

Directions:
Follow signs from the A165 through Filey to the Country
Park.

Facilities:
There is a good washroom, toilets, showers and tumble
driers.

Description:
This a Local Authority owned site overlooking the sea
and is very well looked after with well mown grass, no
litter and well maintained toilet facilities.
A very impressive no-nonsense site. Very tidy, very clean,
not a bad price and great views of the sea.

County:
Yorkshire

Postal town:
Robin Hoods Bay

Address:
Hooks House Farm,
Whitby Road, Robin
Hoods Bay, Whitby,
Yorkshire, YO22 4PE

Telephone number:
01947 880283

E-mail:
jill@hookshousefarm.
holidaylovers.co.uk

Website: www.hooks
housefarm.co.uk

**Ordnance Survey
grid reference:**
NZ-94-945-058

Directions:
From Whitby to Hawkser on the A171 then left on the
B1447 to Robin Hoods Bay for about 2½ miles. The site
is on your right.

Facilities:
Good basic facilities showers, toilets, disposal point,
hook-up.

Description:
The site is in a large gently sloping field which is a part
of a working farm and has glorious views of Robin Hoods
Bay. This is everything good about Yorkshire with a
friendly reception, wonderful views and all at a good
price. In a National Park, this is good walking, cycling
and horse riding country. The site is close to traditional
seaside places such as Scarborough, Robin Hoods Bay
and Whitby and has everything from "Heartbeat"
country, fossils, to Captain Cooks birthplace. Access to
the sea is about a twenty minute walk for the reasonably
fit down hill. However, remember, what goes down must
come back up.

County:
Yorkshire

Postal town:
Whitby

Address:
Sandfield House Farm
Caravan Park, Sandsend
Road, Whitby,
North Yorkshire,
YO21 3SR

Telephone number:
01947 602660

E-mail: info@sandfield
housefarm@.co.uk

Website: www.sandfield
housefarm.co.uk

**Ordnance Survey
grid reference:**
NZ-094-879-116

Directions:
From Whitby travel one mile North on the A174. The site is on the main road on your left opposite Whitby golf course.

Facilities:
Toilets, showers, a laundry, a payphone, electric hook-ups, hard standings and within easy walking distance of Whitby. **The site does not take tents.**

Description:
A twelve acre level site with room for fifty caravans and twenty motor caravans with glorious views of the sea. This site is a good example of how a commercial touring site should be maintained. It is clean and tidy and the grounds are impeccable. The beach is within reasonable walking distance and there are glorious walks with glorious scenery and panoramic views of the sea. On top of this Whitby Abbey is nearby. The park is on the Heritage Coast and in the Yorkshire Moors National Park, there is a steam railway and access to the sea is within a reasonable walking distance.

County:
Yorkshire

Postal town:
Whitby

Address:
Whitby Holiday Parks.
Salt Wick Bay, Whitby.
North Yorkshire,
YO22 4JX

Telephone number:
01947 602664

**Ordnance Survey
grid reference:**
NZ-094-916-108

Directions:
From Scarborough take A171 through Hawkser, turn right following signs to the Y.H.A. The site is on the right 2 miles down the lane.

Facilities:
Toilets, showers, launderette, shops, a take-away and a bar.

Description:
A beautiful, large, tidy commercial site with some statics but most of the cliff top area is given over to tourers. A well run site with not only facilities such as a fish and chip shop but sufficient space to park your caravan far enough away not to be troubled by the alluring smells. It is possible to perch right on the edge of the cliff with glorious views across the sea and is also possible to walk down to the beach if you feel fit enough to walk back up again. Interesting views of Whitby and the Abbey ruins, both of which are close enough to walk to. There are steps down to the sea.

County:
Aberdeenshire

Postal town:
Banff

Address:
Banff Links Caravan
Park, Banff,
Aberdeenshire,
Grampian, AB45 2JJ

Telephone number:
01261 812228

Website: www.aberdeen
shire.gov.uk/caravanpark
s/locations/banff.asp

**Ordnance Survey
grid reference:**
NJ-029-673-645

Directions:
A quarter of a mile off the A98 road one mile West of
Banff. Follow signposts to the site which is on the
seashore.

Facilities:
Superbly kept toilets, showers, electrical hook-ups and a
laundry with an extremely nice children's play area.

Description:
A three and a half acre level site on a low cliff close to
the village with some statics but there are sixty-two
touring pitches most of which have a sea view. There are
twenty-eight touring pitches right on the waterfront and
a safe sandy beach. How remarkable that a local
authority not only owns such a beautiful site but
actually runs it for the benefit of the people. What a
pity other local authorities don't emulate them.
Congratulations to Aberdeen Council. This is a
wonderful tidy site with a very helpful warden, a
beautiful soft sandy safe beach with breakers rolling in
from the sea that you could step into.

County:
Aberdeenshire
A Camping and
Caravanning Club C. S.
Members only

Postal town:
Banff

Address:
Blackpots Cottages,
Whitehills, By Banff,
Aberdeenshire,
AB45 2JN

Telephone number:
01261 861396

**Ordnance Survey
grid reference:**
NJ-029-662-658

Directions:
Two and a half miles West of Banff in Whitehills village.
Continue past a small harbour and around the corner
from a permanent caravan site.

Facilities:
A tap, a chemical disposal point and dustbin.

Description:
A basic C.S. in a small level field with sea views where
you most definitely will need your own sanitation. The
site looks out directly across a rocky beach and the sea
which is just across the road.

County:
Aberdeenshire

Postal town:
Peterhead

Address:
Lido Caravan Park,
South Road, Peterhead,
Aberdeenshire,
AB42 2XX

Telephone number:
01779 473358

Ordnance Survey grid reference:
NK-030-128-453

Directions:
In Peterhead on the seafront by the lido.

Facilities:
Toilets and showers.

Description:
A level site right next to the sea with plenty of electric hook-ups, benches and tables to picnic on. This is a very interesting local authority site with a very helpful warden. There are interesting views and a small harbour. The site, which is extremely well cared for, even has its own little beach and is close to the town and the lido and you really are right next to the beach.

County:
Angus

Postal town:
Monifieth

Address:
Riverview Caravan Park,
Marine Drive, Monifieth,
Dundee, DD5 4NN

Telephone number:
01382 535471

Website: www.ukparks.
co.uk/riverview

**Ordnance Survey
grid reference:**
NO-054-504-322

Directions:
Three miles East of Dundee on the A92 road. In Monifieth turn South off the A930 at the signpost, "Caravan Site." Turn left at the T-junction then first right under a railway bridge with a height restriction of ten feet four inches. The site is one hundred yards further on the left.

Facilities:
Showers, toilets, and a laundry. There is an indoor and outdoors play area and the site is close to the shops.

Description:
A beautifully maintained five and a half acre level site with room for fifty tourers, forty of which have hard-standings and most of which have sea views. A very tidy class site, well looked after with impeccably clean toilets and showers next to an enormous expanse of golden beach. In fact the sea is just over a fence.

County:
Angus

Postal town:
St. Cyrus By Montrose

Address:
Miltonhaven Seaside
Caravan Park, St. Cyrus
(Kincardineshire),
by Montrose, Angus,
DD10 0DL

Telephone number:
01674 850413

E-mail: miltonhaven
@btconnect.com

Website:
www.miltonhaven.co.uk

**Ordnance Survey
grid reference:**
NO-045-775-655

Directions: Two miles North of St. Cyrus. At the crossroads of the A92 and the B9120 turn South East towards the sea. The site is on the right in about half a mile.

Facilities: Toilets, showers, laundry, a recreation room, a play area and farm animals.

Description: A very neat and tidy six acre level site with some statics and fifteen touring pitches most of which have a sea view. This is a very happy little site run by two people with loads of enthusiasm to the task of offering good service. The site has statics, a touring section right on the seashore, its own resident second world war pillbox and a fascinating innovation in the shape of a number of wigwams, built from wood, which children would absolutely love to spend a holiday in. All in all a most enjoyable experience with lovely sea views and friendly chickens. Even for those who would normally never think of playing Bingo the Saturday evening game played here is a great evening's entertainment.

County:
Argyll
A Caravan Club C. S.
Members only

Postal town:
Oban

Address:
North Ledaig Caravan
Club Site, Connel,
Oban, Argyll,
PA37 1RU

Telephone number:
01631 710291

**Ordnance Survey
grid reference:**
NM-049-907-368

Directions:
From Oban on the A85. In Connel turn right onto the A828 signposted Fort William at the crossroads of Connel Bridge taking you under a bridge with a clearance of thirteen and a half feet. You will find the site on the left in about one mile.

Facilities:
All that one would expect of a Caravan Club Site.

Description:
There are panoramic views to the Isle of Mull. The thirty acre park - which has been awarded the David Bellamy Conservation Award - is situated on a two-mile sand and shingle beach on Ardmucknish Bay where sailing, watersports and safe bathing can be enjoyed. Some of the pitches are almost at the water's edge and all pitches face the sea and enjoy a panoramic view to the beautiful Isle of Mull. You can walk along a deserted shoreline to watch wading birds, glimpse an otter or photograph the beautiful sunsets. The site is ideal for children and has a new adventure playground adjacent to the site and if you are on the right pitch you will be able to fall out of bed onto the beach.

County:
Argyll

Postal town:
Oban

Address:
Oban Caravan and
Camping Park,
Gallanachmore Farm,
Gallanch Road, Oban.
Argyll, PA34 4QH

Telephone number:
01631 562425

E-mail: info@oban
caravanpark.com

**Ordnance Survey
grid reference:**
NM-049-830-275

Directions:
From Oban town centre follow the signposts Gallanach.
The site is two and a half miles along the coast road.

Facilities:
Toilets, showers, electric hook-ups, laundry and a shop, a
games room with a pool table and indoor cooking
facilities for campers.

Description:
This is a nine acre site superb for both caravans and
tents on a working farm set alongside the coast road
overlooking the Sound of Kerrera. It is mainly level and
there are some hard standings. This is a very interesting
and attractive site with very helpful staff. There are
beautiful views and it is a very nice place to visit with
masses to do. A great park for children with a sea life
centre, a rare breeds' park and Oban Zoological Park
nearby. It is, of course, great walking country and the
sea is within easy walking distance.

County:
Argyll

Postal town:
Benderloch

Address:
Seaview Camping and
Caravanning Park,
Kielcroft, Benderloch,
Oban, Argyllshire,
PA37 1QS

Telephone number:
01631 720360

**Ordnance Survey
grid reference:**
NM-049-903-387

Directions:
Turn right off the A85 Oban/Connell road onto the
A828 and cross Connell bridge signposted Fort William.
In three miles just past Benderloch village turn left into
the road signposted South Shian/Tralee. The site is on
the left in about five hundred yards.

Facilities:
A toilet block with charges of fifty pence for showers.

Description:
A reasonably level field with some hard standings and a
lovely, quiet peaceful site with views of the bay. A
wonderful place.

County:
Argyll

Postal town:
Tarbert

Address:
Killegruer Caravan Site,
Woodend, Glenbarr,
Tarbert, Argyll,
PA29 6XB

Telephone number:
01583 421241

E-mail: anne@littleson.
fsnet.co.uk

**Ordnance Survey
grid reference:**
NR-068-663-357

Directions:
Turn right off the A83 one mile South of Glenbarr
village. Campbeltown is twelve miles.

Facilities:
Recently upgraded toilets and showers have hand and
hairdriers and include provisions for the disabled. There
are also electric hook-ups. There is a shop and a hotel
nearby.

Description:
The site is mainly set to statics but the touring site has
fifteen pitches right next to the beach. Yet another nice
and comfortable tidy site adjacent to, indeed actually
on, the beach. This is a rather isolated part of the world,
right on the West coast of the Kintyre Peninsula which
suits me down to the ground because that is why I came
to Scotland. The site is within reasonable driving
distance to Campbeltown and you can jump off the site
straight on to the beach.

County:
Argyll

Postal town:
Tarbert

Address:
Muasdale Holiday Park,
Muasdale, Tarbert,
Argyll, PA29 6XD

Telephone number:
01583 421207

Website: www.muasdale
holidays.co.uk

**Ordnance Survey
grid reference:**
NR-068-678-399

Directions:
Follow the A83 South West from Tarbert to Muasdale for about twenty two miles.

Facilities:
Toilets, free showers, a laundrette and dish washing facilities and electric hook-ups. Activities nearby: Golf, Loch fishing, Horse riding. Walks. Scottish Owl Centre. Bird Spotting. There is also a superbly helpful village shop 100 yards from the site.

Description:
A two acre site split in two with statics on one side and pitches for tourers and tents right beside the sea with beautiful views of the islands. Pitches are narrow and tents over 12ft wide will require two pitches for comfort, privacy and to comply with fire regulations. You can jump from your van/tent onto the soft white sand. Ideal location if you are looking for peace and tranquillity, with white beaches and wildlife in abundance. Dinghies, Canoes/Kayaks can be launched from the beach. Sea fishing from beach. Convenient for ferries to Arran, Gigha, Islay and Jura. Dogs welcome.

County:
Argyll

Postal town:
Tayinloan

Address:
Point Sands Holiday
Park, Tayinloan, Argyll,
PA29 6XG

Telephone number:
01583 441263

Website:
www.pointsands.co.uk

**Ordnance Survey
grid reference:**
NR-062-698-484

Directions:
Seventeen miles South of Tarbert on the A83
Campbeltown Road. The site is one mile down a drive
and on the seashore.

Facilities:
Showers, toilets, a payphone and even a hairdrier.

Description:
A level, seventeen acre site overlooking the sea with
absolutely superb views over the bay and islands where
you can pitch directly next to a soft sandy beach and
you could hop from the site on to the beach.

County:
Ayrshire
A Camping and
Caravanning Club Site,
Members only

Postal town:
Maybole

Address:
Culzean Castle Camping
and Caravan Club Club
Site, Maybole,
Strathclyde, KA19 8JX

Telephone number:
01655 760627

**Ordnance Survey
grid reference:**
NS-070-247-103

Directions:
Directions driving from England onto the A719. The site
is four miles on the left.

Facilities:
The normal superb toilets, free showers, a laundrette and
dish washing facilities with electric hook-ups, play area,
dog walk and fully accessible toilets and showers.

Description:
The site is in the grounds of Culzean Castle with superb
views across the sea to the mountains of the Isle of
Arran and is one of a number of Camping and
Caravanning Club sites on the West coast of Scotland
that enjoys the most spectacular sunsets you are ever
likely to see. The coastal scenery is wonderful, the fields
even more so and when we were there we were
entertained by a flock of, what appeared to be, "tame
pheasants" wandering about the other side of the fence.
The sea is about three miles by road.

92

County:
Banffshire

Postal town:
Buckie

Address:
Findochty Caravan Park,
Findochty, Buckie,
Banffshire, Grampian,
AB56 4QA

Telephone number:
01542 835303

E-mail:
moiramain@aol.com

Website: www.findochty
caravanpark.co.uk

**Ordnance Survey
grid reference:**
NJ-028-459-679

Directions:
On the A98 road two miles East of Buckie. Drive to
Findochty harbour and turn left.

Facilities:
Toilets, showers, a payphone and a playground. The site
is on the edge of the village.

Description:
A park of approximately three acres with 16 statics,
some for hire and there are twenty six touring pitches
under the cliffs with electric hook-ups. There are good
views of the Moray Firth. This is a great site, compact
and built into a hollow looking out over the sea and
adjacent to the interesting little town of Findochty and
you can jump into the sea from the site.

County:
Banffshire

Postal town:
Cullen

Address:
Logie Drive, Cullen,
Banffshire, Grampian,
AB56 4TW

Telephone number:
01542 840766

E-mail: enquiries@
cullenbay.co.uk

**Ordnance Survey
grid reference:**
NJ-029-495-683

Directions:
In Cullen off the A98 road and follow signposts to the
site.

Facilities:
Toilets, showers, electrical hook-ups and laundry.

Description:
A four and a half acre level site with caravan holiday
homes and tourers. There are some hard-standings with
sea views. The site is very neat and tidy and has recently
been upgraded to a 4 star park. It is a well cared for site
with an interesting view across the bay and about a
twenty minute walk to the sea.

County:
Banffshire

Postal town:
Portsoy

Address:
Sandend Caravan Park,
Sandend, Portsoy,
Banffshire, Grampian,
AB45 2UA

Telephone number:
01261 842660

E-mail:
sandendholidays@aol.com

Website:
www.thistleparks.co.uk

**Ordnance Survey
grid reference:**
NJ-029-555-663

Directions:
Three miles West of Portsoy, turn North off the A98 road to Sandend. The site is on the right in half a mile adjacent to an old school and a sandy beach.

Facilities:
Toilets and showers revamped in 2006 with one disabled toilet. 10amp hook up. This is a Thistle Parks 4 star site. There is an onsite shop, and shops/pubs two miles both directions. Portsoy two miles away has a slipway for small craft.

Description:
A neat, tidy and level four and a half acre 48 pitch site superbly looked after by the resident owner. Set in a conservation village and over looking the gorgeous flat, golden, sandy beach of Sandend bay with the sea so close you could jump in from the site. Findlater castle is a short walk, with the whisky and castle trails nearby. There are also some first-class golf courses in the area. Open 1st April – 14th October.

County:
Caithness

Postal town:
John O' Groats

Address:
John O' Groats Caravan
and Camping Site,
Caithness, Highlands,
KW1 4YS

Telephone number:
01955 611329

E-mail: info@johno
groatscampsite.co.uk

Website: www.johno
groatscampsite.co.uk

**Ordnance Survey
grid reference:**
ND-012-381-734

Directions:
Situated at the end of the A99 alongside the last house
in Scotland on the seafront.

Facilities:
Toilets, showers, a laundry and a pay telephone.

Description:
A site where you can relax and enjoy panoramic views of
the Pentland Firth, one of the most dangerous shipping
channels in the world with strong ebbing and flowing sea
currents, and spectacular tidal races. You can see the
Island of Stroma, three and a half kilometres from the
mainland, inhabited by a seal colony and the occasional
visitor. You can also see the Orkney Islands from Hoy on
your left and South Walls, Flotta, Swona, South
Ronaldsay and the Pentland Skerries at your extreme
right. Duncansby Head Lighthouse is not far and the
breathtaking views of the Pentland Firth and the Islands
of Orkney and it is only a short walk along the cliff top
to the Long Ceo where you can see Duncansby Stacks
and other magnificent cliff scenery. Grey Seals, often
seen swimming close to the beach." If anyone wants to
say that they have stayed at John O' Groats you will
obviously have to stay on this site. It does have glorious
views.

Photograph from the site manager.

96

County:
Caithness
A Caravan Club C. L.
Non members welcome

Postal town:
Thurso

Address:
Dunnet Bay Caravan
Club Site, Dunnet,
Thurso, Caithness,
KW14 8XD

Telephone number:
01847 821319

**Ordnance Survey
grid reference:**
ND-012-219-705

Directions:
From the East you take the John O'Groats A836 road.
The site is on a roundabout half a mile past the village
of the Dunnet. From the West you take the Thurso A836
road where you will find the site is on your left two and
a half miles past the village of Castletown.

Facilities:
Toilets, showers, a laundry and shops in the village.

Description:
A five acre level site of forty five pitches with many
pitches having glorious views of the sea through the
sand dunes, some right next to it. A good place for
those who like to be solitary, where you can look out
uninterrupted over clean washed sands to Dunnet Head,
the northernmost point of the mainland of Britain. Climb
Dunnet Head for magnificent views over the Pentland
Firth to Orkney, Ben Loyal and Ben Hope. Birdwatchers
can take a ferry trip round the Stacks of Duncansby and
see an amazing range of seabird life. You can repeat
superlatives about Caravan Club Club sites until the
cows come home but the fact is that they are superbly
maintained and managed and this is no exception.

County:
Caithness.
A Caravan Club C. L.

Postal town:
Thurso

Address: 1 West Murkle,
Thurso, Caithness,
Highlands, KW14 8YT

Telephone number:
01847 896405

E-mail: connie
yeomans@ntlworld.com

Ordnance Survey
grid reference:
ND-012-165-693

Directions:
Turn right of the A9 at Thurso onto the A836
signposted Castletown. Within two and three-quarter
miles turn left signposted West Murkle. Within one mile
at a T-junction turn right. Within half a mile turn right
through a gate onto a gravel road across a field to a
second cattle grid gate and the site is on your left.

Facilities:
A tap and chemical disposal point.

Description:
A quarter of an acre secluded site with great sea views. A
wonderful little C. L. in the grounds of a house that is
owned by two very kind people. Access to the sea is two
hundred yards.

County:
Dumfries & Galloway

Postal town:
Annan

Address:
Queensberry Bay
Caravan Park,
Powfoot, Annan,
Dumfries & Galloway,
DG12 5PU

Telephone number:
01461 700205

E-mail: enquiries@
queensberrybay.co.uk

Website: www.queens
berrybay.co.uk

**Ordnance Survey
grid reference:**
NY-085-138-653

Directions:
From Gretna take A75 to Annan then B724,
Annan/Dumfries. Just before Cummertrees turn left
signposted Powfoot. Follow brown caravan and camping
sign, carry on to the end of the road on Solway Firth.

Facilities:
Free hot water, toilets and showers and if that is not
enough there is also a laundry room and a shop with
fresh vegetables.

Description:
This is a working farm but with an attractive entrance to
the site with flowers and mown lawns. The site is in
about a one acre field and has views across the Forth
Estuary. This is a busy and comfortable site with nice
people running it. Very adequate and well cared for with
good facilities. This is an ideal site to start a tour of the
Scottish West and the sea is a one minute walk.

County:
Dumfries & Galloway

Postal town:
Ardwell

Address:
Ardwell Caravan Park,
Ivy Cottage, Ardwell,
Dumfries & Galloway,
DG9 9LS

Telephone number:
01776 860291

**Ordnance Survey
grid reference:**
NX-082-108-456

Directions:
From Glenluce take the A7084 to Ardwell. Look carefully for site notice on the right towards the end of the village.

Facilities:
Showers and toilets.

Description:
A basic site, level with firm ground and a hardcore road through it. A very pleasant, basic, inexpensive site with superb views of the Irish Sea and Luce Bay. You could jump from your caravan into the sea.

County:
Dumfries & Galloway

Postal town:
Dalbeattie

Address:
Sandyhills Bay Leisure Park, Sandyhills, Dalbeattie, Dumfries & Galloway, DG5 4NY

Telephone number:
01387 780257
Bookings on 01557 870267

E-mail: info@sandy hills-bay.co.uk

Ordnance Survey grid reference:
NX-084-890-549

Directions:
Take the A710 coast road from Dalbeattie to Dumfries. The site is on the right at Sandyhills village just past the golf course.

Facilities:
Showers and toilets, a launderette, a shop, a take-away and even a playhouse for children.

Description:
A very well laid out four acre, nicely kept site with trees, a view of the sea and even mountains in the background. This is a really attractive and professionally maintained site with wonderful views of the sea. It has a useful shop and good facilities. The area is dotted with smugglers' coves which are accessible at low tide, there are a number of interesting rock pools and the sea is only a quarter of a mile away.

County:
Dumfries & Galloway

Postal town:
Gatehouse of Fleet

Address:
Auchenlarie Holiday
Park. Gatehouse of
Fleet, Castle Douglas,
Dumfries and Galloway,
DG7 2EX

Telephone number:
01557 840251.

E-mail: enquires@
auchenlarie.co.uk

Website:
www.auchenlarie.co.uk

**Ordnance Survey
grid reference:**
NX-083-536-522

Directions: From Dumfries follow A75 Stranraer until the sign "Gatehouse of Fleet". Continue past town for 5 miles, the Holiday Park is on the left.

Facilities: Toilet and shower block, a 24 hour laundry, indoor heated swimming pool, sports hall, gymnasium, sauna and solarium. An on-site convenience store and a take-away food bar. There is also a private sandy cove, three children's play areas, three licensed bars, resident entertainers, a club with cabaret.

Description:
The touring area is up high with beautiful sea views. Hard standings are available all of which are level and there are also some super pitches. There are four trailer tent pitches with electric hook-ups and four tent pitches on the tenting field. This is a long established remarkably beautifully well cared for site with beautiful sea views. The level of professionalism with which it is maintained puts it among the best in Britain. Their web page is well worth a visit because not only is it one of the best web pages that I have seen but it also contains a mountain of information on the park. The site has its own cove reached by a cliff path.

County:
Dumfries & Galloway

Postal town:
Gatehouse of Fleet

Address:
Mossyard Caravan Park,
Gatehouse of Fleet,
Castle Douglas,
Dumfries & Galloway,
DG7 2ET

Telephone number:
01557 840226

E-mail: enquiry@
mossyard.co.uk

Website:
www.mossyard.co.uk

**Ordnance Survey
grid reference:**
NX-083-546-518

Facilities: Toilets, showers, a laundrette, telephone and a superb social amenity room and boat launching facilities.

Directions: Three-quarters of a mile off the A75 West of Gatehouse.

Description: This is a six and a half acre park mostly level, nicely mown site with most pitches having a view of the sea. Indeed some are right next to it. The site is part of the working farm where the Caravan Park has been operated by its owners for three generations. It is a beautiful place and exceptionally well maintained. It is amongst my best ten sites in Britain and really is worthwhile looking at the web page or sending for a brochure. You could jump from your caravan into the sea.

County:
Dumfries & Galloway
A Caravan Club C. S.
Non members welcome

Postal town:
Port Logan

Address:
New England Bay
Caravan Club Site,
Port Logan, Stranraer,
Wigtownshire, Dumfries
& Galloway, DG9 9NX

Telephone number:
01776 820275

**Ordnance Survey
grid reference:**
NX-082-120-420

Directions:
From the East on the A75 about 2 miles past Glenluce
fork left onto the B7084, signposted Drummore. In
about 6 miles continue onto the A716 signposted
Drummore. The site is on the left in about 6 miles about
one mile past the B7065 junction.

Facilities:
Toilet block, laundry, climbing frame and a games room
all kept to the normal immaculate standards of the
Caravan Club.

Description:
A beautifully set out level site with metalled roads which
will take you to one hundred and fifty individual pitches
with views of the sea. This site is on the edge of Luce
Bay and is carefully landscaped into seven cosy little
areas all with sea views. There is direct access from the
site to a safe, clean and sandy beach which is ideal for
sailing, water sports and sea angling. This an ideal base
for exploring the Forests and Rhins of Galloway, an
unspoilt corner of Scotland. The area has a wealth of
wild flowers and bird life, with a RSPB Visitor Centre, golf
courses, green bowling, pony trekking and a swimming
pool and sports centre in the vicinity. A superb view
across the Bay, the site is adjacent to a beach.

County:
Dumfries & Galloway
A Caravan Club C.L.

Postal town:
Port Logan

Address:
Muldaddie Farm House,
Port Logan, Stranraer,
Dumfries & Galloway,
DG9 9NJ

Telephone number:
01776 860212

**Ordnance Survey
grid reference:**
NX-082-093-403

Directions:
Follow North Stranraer road on A77. Within 1 ³⁄₄ miles continue onto the A716 signposted Drummore. In about 10 miles turn right onto the B7065 signposted Port Logan. Site is through village just past village hall.

Facilities:
Toilet, showers and electric hook-up. The site does not take tents and as the site is affiliated to the Caravan Club it is only open to members.

Description:
A slightly sloping site on a cliff edge overlooking the Bay and Port Logan. A very clean and tidy site with good access and panoramic views across the Bay. An absolutely beautiful site with only a short walk down to Port Logan.

County:
Dumfries & Galloway

Postal town:
Rockcliffe, By Dalbeattie

Address:
Castle Point Caravan
Site. West Barclay Farm,
Rockcliffe,
By Dalbeattie,
Dumfries and Galloway,
DG5 4QL

Telephone number:
01556 630248

**Ordnance Survey
grid reference:**
NX-84-855-532

Directions:
From Dalbeattie take the A710 coastal road. After five
miles turn right along the road signposted to Rockcliffe.
At the brow of the hill just entering Rockcliffe turn left
and drive down to the end of Barclay Road and straight
ahead up a private farm road.

Facilities:
Toilets, showers, hook ups, a laundry and even disabled
toilets.

Description:
A tidy, nicely mown site with real Scottish views of the
sea, islands and mountains. This is very well maintained,
clean and tidy with a helpful site warden. There are
exciting views of the sea and the beach is only a
hundred yards or so. Well worth sending for a brochure.

County:
Dumfries & Galloway

Postal town:
Sandhead

Address:
Sands of Luce Holiday
Park, Sandhead,
Stranraer, Wigtownshire,
Dumfries & Galloway,
DG9 9JN

Telephone number:
01766 830296
and 830456

E-mail: info@sandso
fluceholidaypark.co.uk

Website: www.sandso
fluceholidaypark.co.uk

**Ordnance Survey
grid reference:**
NX-82-102-508

Directions:
From the A75 3 miles West of Glenluce turn South onto
the A716 towards Drummore. Holiday Park is on the left
approaching Sandhead.

Facilities:
Toilet block with free showers, laundry, payphone, shop,
an indoor recreation area and an outdoor playground.

Description:
About a thirty five acre gently sloping site, mainly
holiday homes but with fifty marked pitches for tourers
which are right on the edge of the site with a good sea
view. A site with plenty of facilities that is right on the
edge of a very safe beach with plenty of touring pitches
which are right on the edge of the sea. You could fall
out of bed into the sea.

County:
Dumfriesshire & Galloway
A Caravan Club C.L.

Postal town:
Stranraer

Address:
Hillhead of Craichmore, Leswalt, Stranraer, Dumfriesshire & Galloway, DG9 0PN

Telephone number:
01776 870219

Ordnance Survey grid reference:
NX-082-033-640

Directions:
Leave Stranraer on the A718 Stranraer-Kirkcolm road. In two miles turn right at the roundabout and in about a quarter of a mile turn right into the farm road

Facilities:
A tap, chemical disposal point and electric hook-ups.

Description:
An attractive, level field enclosed by a wall and trees within which is a glorious, traditional, peaceful C.L. with views across the Loch Ryan where you can sit and watch the ferries going to and from Stranraer. Why pay double when you are on your way to catch the ferry. It is about a quarter of a mile to a shingle beach.

County:
East Lothian
A Camping and
Caravanning Club Site

Postal town:
Dunbar

Address:
Barns Ness Camping &
Caravanning Club Site,
Dunbar, East Lothian,
EH42 1PQ

Telephone number:
01368 863536

Website:
www.campingandcaravan
ningclub.co.uk

**Ordnance Survey
grid reference:**
NT-067-723-773

Directions:
On the A1 to Dunbar turn left signposted, Barns Ness
and look for the Camping and Caravanning Club sign on
the right. Turn right and follow a small road to the site
towards the lighthouse.

Facilities:
Toilets, showers, laundry and a play area, washing-up
sinks, chemical disposal point, dog walk and 10 amp
electric hook-ups.

Description:
This is a ten acre level site which is adjacent to a nature
reserve. The Tourist board grade it three star and it has a
three pennon grade from the A.A. As one drives along the
road which takes you to the Barns Ness site, it is so close to
the sea that it possible to miss the site but this guarantees
a superb view. Barns Ness reaches the normal high
standards of the Camping and Caravanning Club with its
very reasonable fees.

County:
East Lothian

Postal town:
Dunbar

Address:
Innerwick, Dunbar, East Lothian, EH42 1QS

Telephone number:
01368 840236

Ordnance Survey grid reference:
NT-067-751-745

Directions:
7 miles South of Dunbar. Turn left, signposted Thornton Loch.

Facilities:
Toilets, washing facilities, electric hook-ups and a site shop.

Description:
A level site right on its own beautiful beach mostly set to statics. This is a lovely little site with a very helpful warden. Primarily the site is for static caravans but a section is set aside with pitches for ten tourers which are provided with hard-standings, a stand pipe close by and electric hook-ups. There are beautiful views of the coastline, it is adjacent to a soft sandy beach, in fact you can step straight onto it and all at a very reasonable price. Pre-booking is advisable.

County:
East Lothian

Postal town:
North Berwick

Address:
Tantallion Caravan and Camping Park, North Berwick, East Lothian, EH39 5NJ

Telephone number:
01620 893348

E-mail: tantallion@ meadowhead.co.uk

Website: www.meadow head.co.uk/tantallon

Ordnance Survey grid reference:
NT-067-566-848

Directions: On the A198 immediately East of North Berwick. From Gullane and take the A198 through North Berwick towards Dunbar. From the A1 turn onto the A198 three miles West of Dunbar.

Facilities: Toilets, free showers, laundry, a games room and a play area.

Description: Tantallion Caravan and Camping Park overlooks the Firth of Forth and is right next to the Glen Golf Course and the beach. It is a level park and is right next to the sea with some holiday homes that are for sale or hire. A truly magnificent site spread across several acres with statics on one side and masses of room for tourers, most with electric hook-ups, all with a glorious view of the sea and the fascinating small islands dotted along the Firth of Forth. This is a beautifully maintained and well kept site with equally well kept facilities at a very reasonable price. It was also a great pleasure to meet such an extremely helpful receptionist. Access to sea is a footpath to the beach.

County:
Fife

Postal town:
Crail

Address:
Sauchope Links Caravan Park, Crail, Fife, KY10 3XJ

Telephone number:
01333 450460

E-mail:
info@sauchope.co.uk

Website:
www.sauchope.co.uk

Ordnance Survey grid reference:
NO-059-624-080

Directions:
Turn right off the Crail/Balcomie road 1 mile North East of Crail.

Facilities:
Toilets, showers and a laundry.

Description:
A neat and tidy twenty acre mostly level site although parts of it are sloping. There are static caravans but there are also fifty touring pitches some with hard-standings and it is right on the edge of the coast. As soon as one enters the site one recognises that it is extremely upmarket. It is beautiful, well cared for and with outstanding views of a rocky coast line. In fact the site is right on the beach.

County:
Fife

Postal town:
Leven

Address:
Monturpie, Upper Largo, Leven, Fife, KY8 5QS

Telephone number:
01333 360254

Ordnance Survey grid reference:
NO-059-433-039

Directions:
Turn off the A915 Upper Largo to St. Andrews Road and in about half a mile turn into the guest house Monturpie where you will find the site.

Facilities:
Toilets, showers and electric hook-ups.

Description:
A slightly sloping, neat and tidy, nicely mown one acre site. We found this attractive site on the top of a hill with a full view across the Firth of Forth. The site is superb with toilets and showers thrown in which must provoke the question, "what more could one ask for?" especially as it is only fifteen minute walk down the hill to a wonderful little village shop. The only drawback, slight as it was, must be "if you walk down a hill you have to walk back up it again". In fact the site is so good that it has had to embark upon a process of extending to meet demand.

County:
Inverness-shire

Postal town:
Arisaig

Address:
Camusdarach Camp
Site, White Sands,
Morar, Arisaig,
Inverness-shire,
PH39 4NT

Telephone number:
01687 400221

E-mail-Address:
CamDarach@aol.com

Website:
Camusdarach.

Ordnance Survey
grid reference:
NM-040-654-894

Directions:
Turn off the A478 North of Largs, 2 miles South of
Wemyss Bay.

Facilities:
Toilets, showers etc in a lovely looking building.

Description:
An attractive, beautifully kept site with wonderful sea
views and with very well cared for grounds. In fact
everything is absolutely pristine and access to the sea is
a very reasonable walk.

County:
Inverness-shire

Postal town:
Arisaig

Address:
Gorten Sands Caravan
Site, Gorten Farm,
Arisaig, Inverness-shire
Highlands, PH39 4NS

Telephone number:
01687 450283

**Ordnance Survey
grid reference:**
NM-040-643-878

Directions:
Leave the A830 one mile North of Arisaig then follow
the "Back of Keppoch" road to the end. The site is
nearly a mile across a cattle grid.

Facilities:
Showers, toilets and electric hook-ups.

Description:
A six acre level site with forty five pitches. A very
pleasant site with good facilities and wonderful views
next a white sandy beach. The site forms part of a
working hill and coastal farm run by the Macdonald
family where traditional harvesting methods are
employed.

County:
Inverness-shire

Postal town:
Arisaig

Address:
Invercaimbe Croft,
Caravan and Camping
Site, Arisaig,
Inverness-shire,
PH39 4NT

Telephone number:
01687 450375

E-mail:
joycew@madasafish.com

Website: www.invercaim
becaravansite.co.uk

Ordnance Survey
grid reference:
NM-040-652-883

Directions:
At Arisaig take the A861. The site is on the left just past "Back of Keppoch."

Facilities:
Electric hook-up points. Laundry room. On site telephones. Toilet, showers and dish washing facilities. It is possible to launch a boat from the site beach with a 4 x 4 and there are temporary moorings available to campers.

Description:
Invercaimbe is a West Highland working croft where traditional Hill Cattle and working Highland Ponies can be found. A lovely little site spread across a couple of acres, most of which is uneven. It is best to check before booking to make sure that a pitch is available especially if you need a flat site. This is a nice basic site with wild views of the mountains behind it and a lovely safe beach in front of it. There are boat trips to all the inner Hebridean islands. Fishing is available on Loch Morar and a pretty nine golf course is situated two miles from the caravan site. Children are usually happy on the beach but if it rains, Mallaig has a good size swimming pool and a marine world. This site is really good value for money and there are some pitches right on the beach.

County:
Inverness-shire

Postal town:
Arisaig

Address:
Portnadoran Caravan Site, Arisaig, Inverness-shire, PH39 4NT

Telephone number:
01687 450267

Ordnance Survey grid reference:
NM-040-650-891

Directions:
On the A830 Fort William to Mallaig Road. Approximately two miles north of Arisaig.

Facilities:
Toilets, showers, dish washing and a laundry.

Description:
The site is right on the edge of a soft white sandy beach and has plenty of level pitches. It overlooks the islands of Skye, Eigg, Rhum and Muck. A wonderful informally managed commercial site and what more could you wish for.

County:
Inverness-shire

Postal town:
Arisaig

Address:
The Croft, "Back of Keppoch", Arisaig, Inverness-shire, PH39 4NS

Telephone number:
01687 450200

E-mail: enquiries@ achnaskiacroft.co.uk

Website:
www.achnaskiacroft.co.uk

Ordnance Survey grid reference:
NM -040-648-879

Directions:
Travel through Arisaig village on the A830. In about two miles turn left at a bus shelter where the caravan site sign is and follow the road until the turning on the right to the farm and site.

Facilities:
Toilets and showers plus electric hook-ups.

Description:
A slightly sloping site but with beautiful views on a working farm in a wonderful part of the world and one can say no better than that.

County:
Inverness-shire
Postal town:
Portnaluchaig

Address:
Silversands Caravan Site,
Portnaluchaig,
Inverness-shire,
Scotland, PH39 4NT

Telephone number:
01687 450269

**Ordnance Survey
grid reference:**
NM-0-653-893

Directions:
On the left of the A830 Fort William-Mallaig road about two and a half miles past Arisaig. Turn left at the caravan and camping site sign.

Facilities:
Toilets and showers.

Description:
A nicely mown, level, lovely little site where the pitches are distributed in little nooks and crannies all over the place providing seclusion for those who want it and access to the sea is only a very short walk.

County:
Mid Lothian
A Caravan Club C. L.
Non members welcome

Postal town:
Edinburgh

Address:
Edinburgh Caravan Club
Site, Marine Drive,
Edinburgh, EH4 5EN

Telephone number:
0131 312 6874

Website:
www.caravanclub.co.uk/UK

**Ordnance Survey
grid reference:**
NT-066-212-768

Directions:
I have put no directions as it is best that you either join the Caravan Club, get them from the Club book or find your own way.

Facilities: Normal superb facilities one gets used to from the Caravan Club.

Description:
Edinburgh Caravan Club Site offers an ideal location for your caravanning holiday. Situated to the North of the city on the Firth of Forth, the site provides easy access to Edinburgh, Europe's festival capital and most beautiful city. In this unique historic setting, you can visit the castle which clings dramatically to the rock, (home to the Scottish Crown Jewels), walk down the Royal Mile to the Palace of Holyrood house (the Queen's official Scottish residence), or enjoy the green expanse of Princes Street Gardens. It is an historic setting - yet Edinburgh is a friendly, modern, cosmopolitan city which has something for everyone all year round. A great site with nice walks about it and a good bus service into Edinburgh. One can get a glimpse of the Firth of Forth from the site which is close to the sea.

County:
Ross-shire

Postal town:
Achiltibuie

Address:
Achnahaird Caravan and Camping Site, Achiltibuie, by Ullapool, Ross-shire, Highlands, IV26 2YT

Telephone number:
01854 622348

Ordnance Survey grid reference:
NC-015-015-136

Directions:
From Ullapool take the A835 North for 10 miles. Turn left at the signpost at Achiltibue onto a single track road for about 12 miles. At T-junction turn right and right again at the Camp Site sign, keep going until you reach a gate on the right with a notice board showing the site prices.

Facilities:
Restaurant and snacks within three miles. Toilets, a chemical disposal point and a tap.

Description:
An enormous, level site with some sloping areas with beautiful views of the sea and the mountains and next to a large sandy beach and what more could one wish for. To find a site at this price with toilets is a boon and I think it's a wonderful place and well worth the long drive. If I say that it is in "my best ten sites in the country" and you find that there are a trifle more than ten sites that I have said that about, so be it.

County:
Ross-shire

Postal town:
Ardmair

Address:
Ardmair Point Caravan Park, Ardmair, Ullapool, Ross-shire, Highlands, IV26 2TN

Telephone number:
01854 612054

E-mail:
sales@ardmair.com

Website:
www.ardmair.com

Ordnance Survey grid reference:
NH-019-109-983

Directions:
Three miles North of Ullapool on the A835 look for a camp site sign by a telephone box.

Facilities:
A shop, electric hook-ups, toilets, showers, laundry, pay phone and a playground.

Description:
A mainly level site right on the sea front. An extremely attractive site with exquisite views, a very safe beach and what a pleasure to find such a helpful person at reception. The site is nearly on the beach.

County:
Ross-Shire

Postal town:
Badcaul Dundonnell

Address:
Northern Lights Campsite, Croft 9, Badcaul, Dundonnell, Ross-shire, IV23 2QY

Telephone number:
There was no telephone line to the site when we stopped there

Ordnance Survey grid reference:
NH-019-024-914

Directions:
From Inverness follow the signs to Ullapool and take the A835 until you come to Braemore Junction. Follow the signs Wester-Ross Coastal Trail A832. Follow the road for approximately 19 miles. You will pass the Dundonnell Hotel on your left. The site is 4 miles past hotel on your right.

Facilities:
Newly refurbished toilets, showers, dishwashing area and electric hook-ups.

Description:
A six acre, neat and tidily mown site for twelve touring caravans or motor caravans and tents with some hard standings. Since the owners moved in they have sympathetically refurbished an old, traditional stone building where the showers and toilets are. I think it is a wonderful little site with wonderful views and enthusiastic owners/managers. Access to sandy beaches is about four miles.

County:
Ross-shire

Postal town:
Dundonnell

Address:
Badrallach, B & B,
Bothy, Cottage and
Campsite, Croft 9
Badrallach, Dundonnell
by Garve. Ross-shire.
Highlands, IV23 2QP

Telephone number:
01854 633281

E-mail: michael.stott2
@virgin.net

Website:
www.badrallach.com

**Ordnance Survey
grid reference:**
NH-019-065-915

Directions:
The approach road is 1 mile East of the Dundonnell
Hotel off the A832 about 7 miles along a single track
road but good passing places.

Facilities:
Free hot water, toilets, showers, a clubroom. B.T.
telephone nearby. Kayaks, Blokarts, Boats, Bikes, Flexifoil
Power Kites and a caravan for hire.

Description:
This a small family run site on the shores of the loch.
There are twelve tent pitches and three pitches for
caravans which must be pre-booked. After all one would
feel a bit of a fool to have driven along this long dead
end road only to find that they are full. This is yet
another site that the owners saw, fell in love with and
bought. In answer to the question, "was the rather long
drive worth it?" I would answer unequivocally, "yes".
Don't go unless you want somewhere absolutely
beautiful, peaceful, tranquil and with an interesting site
owner/manager, his family and Percy a young Clumber
Spaniel. Access to the loch is within easy walking
distance.

Photographs © Michael Stott

124

County:
Ross-shire
A Caravan Club C. L.

Postal town:
Fortrose

Address:
Broomhill Farm, Fortrose,
Ross-shire, Highlands,
IV10 8SH

Telephone number:
01381 620214

**Ordnance Survey
grid reference:**
NH-027-720-569

Directions:
Turn off the A832 in Fortrose signpost Killen. In about
three-quarters of a mile at the top of a hill turn right
into a farm road. The site is on your left in half a mile.
Please call at the farmhouse to book in.

Facilities:
A tap and a chemical disposal point.

Description:
A sloping site at the end of a long farm track at which
you will find a farm that looks as a farm should. There
are gorgeous views. This site has an exciting larger-than-
life panoramic view across the Moray Firth. It is an
amazing place, wild, isolated and totally beautiful and
made even more so by the colony of Bottle Nosed
Dolphins which live in the Firth and can occasionally be
seen with the naked eye and clearly seen with
binoculars.

County:
Ross-shire

Postal town:
Fortrose

Address:
Fortrose Caravan Site,
Harbour Road, Fortrose,
Ross-shire, Highlands,
1V10 8SD

Telephone number:
01381 600217

E-mail: fortrosecaravan
park@hotmail.co.uk

**Ordnance Survey
grid reference:**
NH-027-737-562

Directions:
From Fortrose take the Harbour Road and you will find
the site on your right.

Facilities:
Toilets, showers and electric hook-ups.

Description:
A very pretty, part level, part sloping site right on the
cliffs overlooking the sea with a quiet road behind it. Yet
another beautiful site with a panoramic view of across
the Moray Firth. You could jump into the sea from the
site.

County:
Ross-shire

Postal town:
Gairloch

Address:
Gairloch Caravan and
Camping Holiday Park,
Mihol Road, Strath,
Gairloch, Wester Ross,
Ross-shire, Highlands,
IV21 2BX

Telephone number:
01445 712373

E-mail: info@gairloch
caravanpark.com

Website: www.gairloch
caravanpark.com

**Ordnance Survey
grid reference:**
NG-019-797-774

Directions:
Turn West off the A832 in Gairloch onto the B8021.
Half a mile turn right immediately after the Millcroft
Hotel, the site is on your right.

Facilities:
Electric hook-ups, toilets, hand basins, showers and a
launderette. The site is in a village so shops are quite close.

Description: A beautifully maintained site with eighty
pitches with wonderful views over the sea and towards
the mountains. Very well kept grounds. To cap it all, it's
close to the village with everything you could need for
an interesting stay. This park must be one of the most
peaceful holiday locations in the country surrounded as
it is by superb views of the loch and mountains. It has all
sorts of amenities within close distance and it's well
worth sending for a brochure and the sea is just across
the road.

County:
Ross-shire

Postal town:
Laide

Address: Gruinard Bay Caravan Park, Laide, Wester Ross, Ross-shire, Highlands, IV22 2ND

Telephone number:
01445 731225

E-mail:
gruinard@ecosse.net

Website:
www.highlandbreaks.com

Ordnance Survey grid reference:
NG-019-906-918

Directions:
The Caravan Park is on the A832 about 29 miles from Braemore Junction. Leave Inverness and pass through Contin and Garve, do not take the first turn left and continue twenty miles to Braemore Junction then turn left onto the A832 to Laide where the site is.

Facilities:
Electric hook-ups, free toilets and showers, a shop and close to the village.

Description:
A large open level site right on the sea front with some statics. Yet another site which the current owners liked so much they bought and now manage themselves. The site is largely given over to statics but there are pitches for about forty caravans and/or tents. It is an enjoyable site made the more enjoyable by being able to talk to an owner, who is so enthusiastic about it and you can jump into the sea from the site.

Library Picture

County:
Ross-shire.
A Camping and
Caravannong Club C. S.
Non members welcome

Postal town:
Rosemarkie

Address:
Rosemarkie Camping
and Caravanning Club
Site, Ness Road East,
Rosemarkie, Fortrose,
Ross-shire, Highlands,
IV10 8SE

Telephone number:
01381 621117

Website: www.camping
andcaravanningclub.co.uk

**Ordnance Survey
grid reference:**
NH-027-739-569

Directions: The A832 to Fortrose taking the turning right by the Police Station down Ness Road and first left into a small turning at a Golf Club sign.

Facilities: Immaculately kept toilets, showers including fully accessible facilities, laundry, washing-up facilities and 16 amp electric hook-ups.

Description:
A very attractive level site of sixty pitches right on the beach which has a four star award from the British Tourist Board, three pennons from the A.A and a four star Loo of the year award. This is one of the most beautiful sites in Britain with the normal excellent standards of the Camping and Caravanning Club. There are absolutely stupendous beautiful views looking over the Moray and Cromarty Firths and this spectacular coastline is famous for its Bottlenose Dolphins and it is not too far to walk into a very interesting little town. There is a regular bus service to Inverness. For those individuals addicted to golf I am obliged to state that there is a golf course in very close proximity.

County:
Ross-shire

Postal town:
Ullapool.

Address:
Broomfield Holiday Park,
Shore Street, Ullapool,
Ross-shire, Highlands,
IV26 2SX

Telephone number:
01854 612020 or
01854 612664

E-mail: sross@broom
fieldhp.com

Website:
www.broomfieldhp.fsnet.
co.uk/contact_us.htm

**Ordnance Survey
grid reference:**
NH-019-125-938

Directions:
In Ullapool continue along Shore Street and take the second right after the harbour where you will see a wide site entrance on the left.

Facilities:
Showers, toilets, a launderette and a children's playground.

Description:
A large level field overlooking the sea. Tidy, clean and close to village amenities. Broomfield Holiday Park is a family run site set on the banks of Lochbroom in Ullapool, looking out to the Summer Islands and Hebrides. For anyone wishing to tour and camp in the Highlands of Scotland, Broomfield offers a well maintained and serviced site, centrally located for many of the most popular Highland destinations, and set in an outstanding environment famed for scenery and sunsets alike. This is a very nice site with some extraordinary beautiful views, good facilities and the sea is just across the road.

County:
Sutherland

Postal town:
Dornoch

Address:
Grannie's Helian' Hame,
Embo, Dornoch,
Sutherland, Highlands,
IV25 3QD

Telephone number:
01862 810383
Bookings 0870 9904136

E-mail:
customerrelations
@parkdeanholidays.com

Website: www.parkdean
holidays.co.uk

**Ordnance Survey
grid reference:**
NH-021-818-926

Directions:
A9/A949 road to Dornoch. Take the unclassified road
North for two and a half miles and turn right into Embo.

Facilities:
Toilets, showers, laundrette, shop, pub, restaurant and
takeaway. There are 220 touring pitches of which 120
have electric hook-ups.

Description:
A large site with loads of facilities set amongst sand
dunes with a large play area and adventure playground.
When I saw this site in the Caravan and Camping Club
"Big Site Book", I was not looking forward to visiting it
because I do not like large sites but this one is rather
different. The touring pitches are based on the edge of
the site with plenty of space and many of those with the
electric hook-ups are right on the edge of the beach and
the prices are really very reasonable. The site is also
within walking distance to a small village.

County:
Sutherland

Postal town:
Durness

Address:
Sango Sands Caravan
and Camping Site,
Durness, Sutherland,
Highlands,
IV27 4PP

Telephone number:
01971 511262/511726

E-mail:
Keith.durness
@btinternet.com

**Ordnance Survey
grid reference:**
NC-009-405-678

Directions:
On the A838 in Durness village overlooking Sango Bay.

Facilities:
Toilets, showers, a drying room and laundry. Handy to
the village shop and other amenities such as a bar and
restaurant.

Description:
A part level, part sloping field of about ten and a half
acres with lovely views of the beach. A large wonderful
sprawling site spread across ten and a half acres which
allows you to find little nooks and crannies to hide in.
You can even park on the cliff with a near sheer drop to
the sea below you. There are good facilities. It was nice
to find staff who were willing to share their local
knowledge with you but the nicest bit was to be able to
lay in bed and listen to the sea pounding on the rocks
which is a one minute walk away.

County:
Sutherland

Postal town:
Lairg

Address:
Scourie Caravan and
Camping Park, Harbour
Road, Lairg, Sutherland,
Highlands, IV27 4TG

Telephone number:
01971 502060

**Ordnance Survey
grid reference:**
NC-009-154-446

Directions:
On the A894 in Scourie overlooking Scourie Bay twenty
six miles from Durness and forty five miles from Ullapool.

Facilities:
Toilets, free showers and a laundry, nearby launching
slip, restaurant at the entrance to the site and the village
is only a short walk.

Description:
A four acre site with good view of the bay and sixty
pitches on level ground with some hard standings. The
site has good facilities, is well laid out, very tidy and
close to the shops and beach. The water is exceptionally
clear and free of pollution which makes it ideal for skin
diving. Golden eagles, deer otter, badgers, wildcat and
pine martins are native to the area and seals can be seen
at locations nearby and on top of that it is great hill
walking country.

County:
Sutherland

Postal town:
Lochinver

Address:
Shore Caravan Site,
106 Achmelvich,
Lochinver, Sutherland,
Highlands, IV27 4JB

Telephone number:
01571 844393

E-mail: enquiries@
shorecaravansite.co.uk

Website: www.shore
caravansite.co.uk

**Ordnance Survey
grid reference:**
NC-015-055-248

Directions:
On the A837 half a mile before Lochinver turn right onto the B869 signposted Stoer, Drumbeg, Achmelvich. In 1½ miles turn left signposted Achmelvich for 1½ miles. In the village go past telephone box straight onto site about 250 yards at the end of the road.

Facilities:
Toilets, showers, electric hook-ups, a launderette, pay phone, shop with groceries, ice creams, cold drinks and a fish and chip takeaway.

Description:
A large part level, part sloping site with some hard standings. If you want a sea view you must make sure that one is available when you book in. A large and attractive site with plenty of space, very good facilities and beautiful sea views and the site is adjacent to the beach.

County:
Anglesey

Postal town:
Amlwch

Address:
Point Lynas Caravan Park,
Llaneilian, Amlwch,
Isle of Anglesey,
LL68 9LT

Telephone number:
01407 831130 or
01248 852423

E-mail:
enquiries@pointlynas.com

Website:
www.pointlynas.com

**Ordnance Survey
grid reference:**
SH-114-474-929

Directions: Take the A5025 from the 2nd exit after the Britannia Bridge signposted, Bellech Amlwch. After 15 miles at Cerrig Man turn right at Anglesey Mowers then after ³/₄ miles turn right at the T-junction. Pass the church on your left and sharp left at the end of a short straight. Pass the telephone box and the park entrance is three hundred yards on your left.

Facilities: Toilets, laundry with washing machine and drier, wet suit washing area. A baby bath and a changing mat are also provided.

Description: Pitches for seventeen touring caravans in two separate fields set aside just for tourers. One has serviced hard standings and the other has level grass pitches but all pitches have electric hook-ups. A beautifully cared for site. Most of the pitches have panoramic views of the sea and lighthouse. On a good day you can see the Isle of Man. The park is beautiful and there are all manner of interesting things to do and to see within easy reach, such as the Anglesey Coastal footpath which can be walked seven miles in each direction. Access to the sea, a five minute walk.

County:
Anglesey

Postal town:
Dulas

Address:
Tyddyn Isaf Caravan Park, Lligwy Bay, Dulas, Isle of Anglesey, LL7 9PQ

Telephone number:
01248 410203

E-mail: Enquiries@ tyddynisaf.demon.co.uk

Website: www.tyddynisaf. demon.co.uk

Ordnance Survey grid reference:
SH-114-486-874

Directions:
As you enter the Isle of Anglesey on the A5025 take 2nd turning after Britannia bridge signposted "Bellech-Amlwch" then take the A 5025 through Bellech and at the 1st roundabout turn left and continue to a telephone box where you turn right. The site is half a mile down the line.

Facilities:
Toilets, showers, hairdryer, laundry room, clubhouse, restaurant.

Description:
A highly professionally set out and managed site with a high level of cleanliness everywhere. A superb children's play area and the site is mostly level with views of the sea. There was also the mark of a quality site in that an electric hook up and even a tap had been placed in the late arrival place. A beautiful site with panoramic views across the sea. A wonderful safe place for children with a good variety of play equipment and a gorgeous beach with easy access.

Library Picture

County:
Ceredigion

Postal town:
Aberystwyth

Address:
Morfa Bychan, Holiday
Park, Llanfarian,
Aberystwyth,
Ceredigion,
SY23 4QQ

Telephone number:
01970 617254

**Ordnance Survey
grid reference:**
SN-135-568-772

Directions:
From Aberystwyth on the A 487 heading South to
Blaenplyf take the first turning right after the village site.
It is best to approach the site from Blaenplyf rather than
Rhydefelin.

Facilities:
A small shop, a heated swimming pool, toilets, showers,
hook-ups, an indoor amusement room and outdoor
children's play areas.

Description:
A beautifully laid out six acre site, slightly sloping. Very
clean and with glorious views overlooking Cardigan Bay
and with views across unspoilt farmland for as far as I
could see. A beautiful, extremely well maintained site
with beautiful views and very close to the sea.

County:
Ceredigion

Postal town:
New Quay

Address:
Cei Bach Country Club,
Parc-y-Brwcs Cei Bach,
New Quay, Ceredigion,
SA45 9SL

Telephone/Fax
Number:
01545 580237

E-mail: paul@ceibach.
freeserve.co.uk

Website:
www.cei-bach.co.uk

Ordnance Survey
grid reference:
SN-146-408-595

Directions:
From the A487 coast road take the B4342 road at
Llanarth signposted New Quay. Approximately two miles
opposite the Cambria Hotel turn right signposted
Cei Bach. In about one mile after crossing a stone bridge
turn left at a T-junction and left at a signpost Traeth
Bach, Cei Bach Camp Site is fifty yards on the left.

Facilities:
Launderette, washing up area, ironing and chemical
disposal point and free showers. Club house, bar, games
room, and play park.

Description:
Beautifully kept, slightly sloping field. It is not surprising
that this site received two major awards as the best
camping site in Wales from the A.A. and Practical
Caravan Magazine. It is a beautifully maintained site.
Booking is essential in peak season and access to a
sandy beach is 200 yards.

© Mr & Mrs Dent

County:
Conwy

Postal town:
Colwyn Bay

Address:
Bron-Y-Wendon Caravan
Park, Wern Road,
Llanddulas, Colwyn Bay,
Conwy, LL22 8HG

Telephone number:
01492 512903

E-mail: bron-y-wendon
@northwales-holidays.co.uk

Website:
www.northwales-
holidays.co.uk

**Ordnance Survey
grid reference:**
SH-116-903-785

Directions: Take the A55 into North Wales leaving at the Llanddulas interchange, junction 23. Turn first right following tourist signs to the caravan park.

Facilities: Two centrally heated toilet blocks with the most up to date facilities. There are also designated fully accessible facilities with grade two access. A fully-fitted laundry, a games room with table tennis and satellite television channels. Public telephone, gas sales and Broadband Internet Access with Computer Hotspots.

Description:
A level and very well kept park of one hundred and thirty pitches set in small groups, every one of which has a beautiful coastal view overlooking the sea towards Colwyn Bay and beyond to the Orme at Llandudno. The sea and beach are just a short walk away and the village of Llanddulas has shops and good pubs. Nearby there are a range of leisure activities including swimming, golf, fishing, horse riding and water sports. Open all year but no tents allowed.

County:
Conwy

Postal town:
Penmaenmawr

Address:
Tyddyn Du Touring Park,
Conwy Old Road,
Penmaenmawr, Conwy,
North Wales, LL34 6RE

Telephone number:
01492 622300

E-mail: stay@tyd
dyndutouringpark.co.uk

Website: www.tyddyn
dutouringpark.co.uk

Ordnance Survey
grid reference:
SH-115-730-770

Directions: Take the A55 West from Conwy for 5 miles. Then take the 1st left at the new roundabout after the Little Chef Restaurant. Immediately afterwards turn left and the site entrance is on the right after a golf course.

Facilities: An immaculate toilet block, a utility room including a tumble drier an iron and ironing board and Belfast sink for washing clothes.

Description:
A beautiful **ADULTS ONLY** site with panoramic views across Conway Bay to the Great Orme at Llandudno and over to Anglesey and Puffin Island. The park is within a few yards of Snowdonia National Park with loads of great walks. When I visited the park there was all sorts of work being done to it to improve it even more. Plenty of level pitches, tarmac roads and every pitch has a sea view. A beautiful site, beautiful panoramic views across Conway Bay and only a short walk to the sea. If you open their web page and click onto "Panorama" you will get a superb tour of the park.

County:
Gwynedd

Postal town:
Aberdaron

Address:
Morfa Mawr Farm,
Aberdaron, Pwllheli,
Gwynedd, North Wales,
LL53 8BD

Telephone number:
01758 760264

**Ordnance Survey
grid reference:**
SH-123-183-262

Directions:
From Aberdaron take the coastal road signposted Rhiw.
The site is the first turn on the right-hand side.

Facilities:
Toilets and a disposal point.

Description:
A three acre partly sloping, partly level site with idyllic
views across Aberdaron Bay to the headland, Bardsey
Sound. There are glorious sea views and it is only five
minutes or so to the beach.

County:
Gwynedd

Postal town:
Aberdaron

Address:
Myndd Mawr Camping and Caravan Site, Enquiries to: Carol and Robert Jones, Llanllawen Fawr, Aberdaron, Pwllheli, Gwynedd, LL53 8BY

Telephone number:
01758 760223

E-mail: llanllawen@uwchm ynydd.freeserve.co.uk

Website: www.aberdaron caravanandcampingsite.co.uk

Ordnance Survey grid reference:
SH-123-158-248

Directions:
From Aberdaron take the St. Mary's Well road. Follow the road sign Uwchmyndd. The site is on the left 1½ miles from Aberdaron at the end of the road. A map of how to get to the site is at the bottom of the tariff page of the web site.

Facilities:
Toilets and showers and two miles from Aberdaron which has pubs, shops and a church. A seafood restaurant ¼ of a mile from the site.

Description:
Beautiful and one of my top ten sites on the British coast. Two flat very nicely mown fields, slightly sloping in some places where there are even picnic tables. A glorious isolated site overlooking the Bardsey Peninsular. An area of outstanding natural beauty with views to the historic and beautiful Bardsey Island. There is certainly a good view of the sea and there are a number of footpaths which lead through the adjoining headland to the rocky coastline which meet the waters of Bardsey Sound.

County:
Gwynedd
A Caravan Club C. L.
Members only

Postal town:
Aberdaron

Address:
Plasffordd, Aberdaron,
Pwllheli, North Wales,
LL53 8LL

Telephone number:
01758 760439

**Ordnance Survey
grid reference:**
SH-123-163-284

Directions:
Fork right off the B 4413 (Llanbedrog- Aberdaron) about ³/₄ of a mile past Pen-Y-Groeslon (B4417) Junction. In ¹/₄ of a mile past Aberdaron boundary sign fork right by the council houses and the site is in one mile.

Facilities:
Toilets and shower.

Description:
A three quarter of an acre flat site with distant chocolate box views of the sea. A nice quiet secluded place with very nice views and at very reasonable prices. Access to the sea is about one mile to a sandy beach called Whistling Sands.

County:
Gwynedd

Postal town:
Aberdaron

Address:
Ty-Newydd Farm Caravan and Camping Site, Uwchmynydd, Aberdaron, Pwllheli, Gwynedd, North Wales, LL53 8BY

Telephone number:
01758 760581

E-mail: www.tynewydd farm.site.co.uk

Ordnance Survey grid reference:
SH-123-146-257

Directions:
From Aberdaron take the St. Mary's Well road. Follow the road signposted Uwchmyndd. The site is on the left 1 ½ miles from Aberdaron.

Facilities:
Showers, toilets with very generous cubicles. There are also washing-up facilities and a children's play area.

Description:
Two flat fields with a hardcore road through the first field. There are a number of hard standings. This is a very tidy and well cared for site very reasonably priced with a lovely view overlooking Bardsey Island in one of the most beautiful settings one can find in Britain. There is an added bonus that the sandy beach is only one and a half a miles away or so.

County:

Gwyned

Postal town:
Clynnog Fawr

Address:
Aberafon Camp Site,
Gyrn Goch, Clynnog Fawr,
Caenarfon, Gwyned,
North Wales, LL54 5PN

Telephone number:
01286 660295

E-mail:
hugh@maelor.demon.co.uk

Website:
www.maelor.demon.co.uk

**Ordnance Survey
grid reference:**
SH-123-400-485

Directions:
The A487 to Llanwnda where you fork right onto the
A499. Site is 1 mile South of Clynnog Fawr on main
road. Turn right at the red shed.

Facilities:
Toilets, showers and hook-ups.

Description:
A fifteen acre part level site with sea views adjacent to
its own private beach. An attractive site with access for
boats and superb countryside and to add to that it is
only twenty minutes from Snowdon. Some pitches are so
close to the beach one could throw a pebble onto it.

County:
Gwynedd

Postal town:
Llangwnnadl

Address:
Llecyn, Llangwnnadl,
Pwllheli, Gwynedd,
North Wales,
LL53 8NT

Telephone number:
01758 770347

**Ordnance Survey
grid reference:**
SH-123-196-336

Directions:
From Pwllheli take the A4972 Morfa Nefyn. Then take the B4412 through Eden Tudweiliog and Llangwnnadl. Take the first right off the main road towards Porth Colman. The site is ¾ of a mile from Porth Colman.

Facilities:
Showers, toilet disposal, laundry facilities and hook-ups.

Description:
A four acre level and very nice tidy site with very reasonable prices and beautiful views of the sea. If you get fed up with the sea you can watch the even more beautiful horses in the nearby field and access to the sea is only about a fifteen minutes walk.

County:
Gwyned

Postal town:
Tywyn

Address:
Cae-Du, Rhoslefain,
Tywyn Gwynedd,
LL36 9ND

Telephone number:
01654 711234

**Ordnance Survey
grid reference:**
SH-124-570-060

Directions:
A493 from Aberdory through Tywyn, Bryn-crug and Rhoslefain. Quarter of a mile after Rhoslefain there is a very sharp right hand bend. Turn left on the bend to the farm house. Book in before proceeding.

Facilities:
Electric hook-ups, toilets, showers, laundry room, disposal point, taps and water from a spring.

Description:
The site is right on the edge of a glorious beach and is the most idyllic site one could ever wish for and fits straight into my best ten sites in Britain. Access is a trifle tight but we got our 6m motorhome down the rather rough and steep track and under a railway bridge. As you come out from under the bridge you are suddenly exposed to the most beautiful coastline on either side that you are ever likely to see, and I can quite believe the farmer who owns the site when he told me that he recently had a group from Switzerland who came to stay for one night and stayed for a month. You can roll out of bed into the sea if you wish to.

County:
Monmouthshire

Postal town:
Portskewett

Address:
St. Pierre Caravan Park,
Portskewett, Nr. Chepstow,
Monmouthshire,
NP6 4TT

Telephone number:
01291 425114.

**Ordnance Survey
grid reference:**
ST-162-510-895

Directions:
Exit the M48 at junction 2 and take the A466 road towards Chepstow. At the first roundabout take the exit to the A48 towards Newport and travel for approximately two miles to a roundabout where you turn left for Portskewett and the site is two hundred and fifty yards on the left.

Facilities:
Showers and toilets, electric hook-ups, dishwashing sinks, disabled facilities. A fully equipped gymnasium and a boule alley.

Description:
The site is between the two bridges leading to and from Wales with views over the Bristol Channel and it is possible to walk down to Black Rock. A very clean and tidy, well kept site with beautiful views across the Bristol Channel with the benefit of being in a village with pubs and restaurants.

County:
Pembrokeshire

Postal town:
Bosherston

Address:
Trefalen Farm,
Bosherston,
Pembrokeshire,
SA71 5DR

Telephone number:
01646 661643

E-mail:
trefalen @.force9.co.uk

**Ordnance Survey
grid reference:**
SR-158-974-939

Directions:
The B4319 from Pembroke. Go through Bosherston village, past the church on your left, and turn left just past St. Govan's Country Inn signposted 'Broadhaven'. The site is one mile on the right near the white farmhouse just before the road ends.

Facilities:
Toilet, waste disposal and battery re-charging facilities and a tap. Open all year.

Description:
A beautiful field ideal for those looking for peace and remoteness only 100 metres from the unspoilt, sandy beach of Broadhaven one of the most outstanding and safe beaches on the Pembrokeshire coast. The surrounding cliffs are internationally renowned within the rock-climbing fraternity and provide breath-taking sea views. Easy walking distance of Barafundle bay, Stackpole harbour and woods and the famous Bosherston Water Lily Ponds with their wealth of unusual wildlife, birds, rare plants and coarse fishing. Otters, kingfishers, herons and large pike are often to be seen. An absolutely breathtaking view.

County:
Pembrokeshire

Postal town:
Saundersfoot

Address:
Trevayne Caravan and
Camping Park,
Monkstone,
Saundersfoot,
Pembrokeshire,
SA69 9DL

Telephone number:
01834 813402

Website:
www.camping-
pembrokeshire.co.uk

**Ordnance Survey
grid reference:**
SN-158-139-030

Directions:
From Carmarthen take the A40 to St. Clears, A477 to
Kilgetty then A478 SP Tenby. At New Hedges turn left
onto B4316 entrance and the park is next turning on
left.

Facilities:
Sixty pitches, hook-ups, showers and shaver points.

Description:
This is a working farm site with five fields providing two
hundred and fifty pitches on grass, partly sloping in the
Pembrokeshire National Park. It is only a fifteen minute
walk to New Hedges village where there are two
restaurants, a pub, a petrol station and a Post Office.
The site has grand views and the farmer who owns the
site was hard at it the day we were there harrowing a
field prior to sowing it with barley, so people with
children must take the appropriate safety measures. The
park is situated in the Pembrokeshire National Park,
Britain's only coastal National Park, and it has its own
private secluded beach called Monkstone Bay which is
ideal for bathing, boating and fishing. It has its own
sandy beach, a fifteen minute walk downhill but
remember you have to come back up it.

County:
Pembrokeshire

Postal town:
St. David's

Address:
Caerfai Bay Caravan and
Tent Park, St. David's,
Haverford West,
Pembrokeshire,
SA62 6QT

Telephone number:
01437 720274

E-mail:
info@caerfai bay.co.uk

Website:
www.caerfaibay.co.uk

**Ordnance Survey
grid reference:**
SM-157-755-250

Directions:
Half a mile South of St. David's off the coast road to
Caerfai Bay.

Facilities:
Immaculate toilets, showers, a bath for small children,
laundry, dishwashing and laundry machines. Even the
elsan emptying points had hand washing and drying
facilities next to them.

Description:
Ten acres part level part sloping fields with a good
number of level pitches. The site is beautifully mown and
tended. As we moved along this coast we often thought
that we had reached the ultimate site but for me this is
as close to the ultimate site that it is possible to find. It
is a family owned and run site, well kept and maintained
with a very considerate staff and the most beautiful
views that we have yet seen with small islands dotted
about in the sea. There was even a herd of happy
looking cows in the field next to us looking over the
fence and access to the sea is only a couple of hundred
yards.

County:
Pembrokeshire

Postal town:
St. Davids

Address:
Rhosson Ganol and
Rhosson Isaf Farm,
St. Davids,
Haverford West,
Pembrokeshire,
SA62 6PY

Telephone number:
01347 720361

**Ordnance Survey
grid reference:**
SM-157-725-250

Directions:
On the A 487 to St. David's, 1½ miles West to the site along the road to the lifeboat station opposite the tip of Ramsey Island.

Facilities:
Toilet, showers, tap and electric hook-ups.

Description:
A six acre touring site spread over two fields with level pitches for six caravans. Peak booking is essential. There are fantastic views of the sea, Ramsey Island and rolling countryside on a site which is also a working farm and access to the sea is only about a ten minute walk.

County:
Pembrokeshire

Postal town:
Tenby

Address:
Windmills Camping Park,
Old Narbeth Road,
Tenby, Pembrokeshire,
SA70 8TJ

Telephone number:
01834 842200

**Ordnance Survey
grid reference:**
SN-158-128-012

Directions:
Off the A4139 three and a half miles South West of
Tenby.

Facilities:
Clean and tidy toilets and showers.

Description:
A five acre site field that is pretty level with very good
sea views over Tenby and Caldey Island with footpath
and cycle tracks to Tenby and the beach. This is a good,
homely site with good sea views and close enough to go
to all sorts of interesting places and only about twenty
minutes gentle walk to the sea.

County:
Swansea

Postal town:
Penmaen

Address:
Nicholaston Farm,
Caravan and Camping
Site, Penmaen, Swansea,
SA3 2H

Telephone number:
01792 371209

Website: www.nicholas
tonfarm.co.uk

**Ordnance Survey
grid reference:**
SS-159-516-884

Directions:
M4 exit 42, A483 Swansea along Fabian Way. Left at the
traffic lights over the River Tawe. Left onto the A4067,
"South Gower and Port Eynon". Follow road 3 ½ miles to
Black Pill, pass outdoor paddling pool on left and
"Woodman" pub on right. Take right-hand lane and turn
right onto B4436 signposted "South Gower & Port
Eynon". At the junction, continue for 4 miles and turn
left onto the A4118. Penmaen is situated between the
villages of Parkmill and Nicholaston. When entering
village of Nicholaston look for the sign "Beynons" and
turn left into a concrete road to the first farm. There are
no signs but go into farmyard and the reception area is
on the left.

Facilities:
Spotless, spacious toilets and showers. Laundry and
chemical disposal. Use of freezer.

Description:
Sloping but some flat surfaces. A very neat and tidy
working farm, indeed they were getting ready to plant
potatoes the day we visited. Friends have been telling us
to come to the Gower for years and how right they were.
This is absolutely superb. Idyllic surroundings with
glorious views of the bay. Peaceful and quiet and access
to the sea is directly from the site.

County:
Swansea

Postal town:
Penmaen

Address:
Three Cliffs Bay Caravan
Site, North Hills Farm,
Penmaen, Gower,
Swansea, SA3 2HB

Telephone number:
01792 371218

**Ordnance Survey
grid reference:**
SS-159 525-884

Directions: From the M4 take exit number 42 to the A483 towards Swansea along Fabian Way. Turn left at the traffic lights over River Tawe. Turn left onto the A4067, signposted, "South Gower Port Eynon". Follow this road for three and a half miles to Black Pill passing an outdoor paddling pool on the left and "The Woodman" pub on the right. Take the right-hand lane and turn right onto the B4436 signposted "South Gower & Port Eynon". At the junction after four miles turn left onto the A4118. Penmaen is situated between Parkmill and Nicholaston on the left-hand side of the road.

Facilities: Washing up facilities, toilets, showers, chemical disposal point, battery charging and ice pack freezing. All the facilities are spotlessly clean.

Description: There is some level ground but it is mostly sloping with absolutely idyllic view of Three Cliffs Bay. This is an absolutely beautiful site with spotless showers and a lovely well stocked shop. It was a sheer joy to lie in the motor caravan and be rocked to sleep by a gentle, warm sea breeze and then wake up and look out on this, one of the most beautiful coastlines in the world.

Index of Camping and Caravan Sites by Site and Park Name

Please use this form to update the site information in this guide. We particularly need good photographs that represent the site and where possible show the sea view. Nominations for new sites are very welcome.

Site Name:

Address:

Postcode:

Tel. No.

Email:

Website:

Opening and closing dates:

OS grid:

GPS Reference in the following format: N49°14.988' W000°16.838'

Directions:

Pitches: Acres:

RV's taken: yes ☐ no ☐   Dogs allowed: yes ☐ no ☐
                                                            tick as applicable

Please see overleaf

Features:

Hook-up:

Toilets:

Disabled WC:

Showers:

Washing up:

Laundry:

Awards affiliation:

Other features:

Onsite Shop:

Nearest Shops:

Pub:

Slipway:

Description:

Photograph(s) submitted:

Please detach form and post to: Vicrious Books, PO Box 72, Minehead, TA24 9AL